ACA Simplified

Advanced Level Financial Reporting Exam Room N

**ICAEW
PARTNER IN
LEARNING**

Recognised as an ICAEW Partner in Learning, working with ICAEW in the professional development of students

ICAEW takes no responsibility for the content of any supplemental training materials supplied by the Partner in Learning.

The ICAEW Partner in Learning Logo, ACA and ICAEW CFAB are all registered trademarks of ICAEW and are used under licence by ACA Simplified.

A Reminder About Copyright

Please do not photocopy or otherwise distribute this book. Copyright theft is a clear breach of professional ethics and may therefore be reported to ICAEW. We have put a considerable amount of time and effort into developing innovative materials which we genuinely feel will give you an edge in the exams. We would be grateful if you would respect these efforts by not copying this text.

Copyright © 2019 ACA Simplified. All rights reserved.

No part of this publication may be reproduced, stored in a retrieval system or transmitted in any form or by any means without the prior written permission of ACA Simplified.

Disclaimer

The text in this book does not amount to professional advice on any particular technical matter and should not be taken as such. No reliance should be placed on the content as the basis for any investment or other decision or in connection with any advice given to third parties.

ACA Simplified expressly disclaims all liability for any losses or other claims, whether direct, indirect, incidental, consequential or otherwise arising in relation to the use of these materials.

We have made every effort to ensure that the materials are accurate and free from error. Please inform us immediately if you believe that you have discovered any problems with the text.

Whilst we strongly believe that our learning materials are an effective method of preparing for your examinations, ACA Simplified does not accept any liability whatsoever for your ultimate performance in the examination as a result of using this text.

Other ACA Simplified Resources for CR and SBM (and a discount!)

In addition to this book, we provide a range of other study resources for CR and SBM.

On-Demand Video Tuition

Our popular on-demand video courses provide a convenient way to obtain expert tutor guidance for CR and SBM. Our courses can be viewed at any time and as often as you wish – perfect for revising the tricky technical areas of the syllabus!

Our courses contain advice on examination technique, planning methods and time management. We also provide a large number of Tutor Talkthroughs of past paper, Question Bank and ICAEW Mock questions, helping you to identify the patterns in terms of what is rewarded in the model answer each time a topic is tested. This method of reviewing model answers in "batches" of examples on the same topic can be very effective as it teaches you what the examiners are going to be looking for every time. We also review the mark allocation in past paper answers so that you can understand how to allocate your time effectively.

As a thank you for purchasing this book, we are delighted to offer you a **10% discount on the 2019 edition of our CR or SBM on-demand courses (or both!)**. Simply email us with your proof of purchase for this book and we will be in touch to explain how to obtain discounted access to the relevant course(s). For administrative and technical reasons, this offer is only available if you contact us **before** purchasing your on-demand course(s): **retrospective discounts will not be provided**. Your discount request must be received no later than 30 June 2019 (in respect of the July 2019 sitting) and no later than 15 October 2019 (in respect of the November 2019 sitting). This offer is limited to one discount per course per original purchaser of this book: no discount will be provided on any second-hand purchase of the book. No cash alternative will be provided. This offer is not available to students on our classroom CR or SBM tuition courses as access to our on-demand courses is already provided for free as part of our classroom course fee. We regret that we cannot make this offer available to any students whose access to our on-demand courses is paid for by their employer: our offer is only available to students who are purchasing in a personal capacity. Please allow 5 working days for access instructions to be sent by email. All other aspects of the discount are subject to our reasonable discretion and the offer may be withdrawn at any time without notice.

For further information on our on-demand courses, including a free video explanation of how the courses work, please see our website at **www.acasimplified.com**.

Further Study Books and Exam Room Notes

We produce interactive, self-test Q&A books for Advanced Level Financial Reporting and Advanced Level Audit and Assurance. We have condensed and simplified the syllabus content into hundreds of short-form questions that help you learn by testing yourself – much more effective than trying to learn simply by reading from the page or making notes. Our Q&As provide an ideal way to build your technical knowledge so that you can then attempt full exam-standard questions on the basis of a firmer foundation of understanding.

In addition to this set of Exam Room Notes for Financial Reporting, we provide a set of Exam Room Notes covering Audit & Assurance for the Advanced Level. Our *Audit & Assurance Exam Room Notes* book covers not only audit risks & procedures but also provides quick reference notes on specialist assurance areas such as Corporate Governance, internal auditing, social and environmental auditing, and other areas. *Our Audit & Assurance Exam Room Notes* therefore provide you with coverage for all types of audit and assurance question in both CR and SBM.

Other ACA Simplified Resources for CR and SBM (and a discount!)

Our *Strategic Business Management Exam Room Notes* provide reminder notes on over 100 key SBM topics such as acquisitions, valuations, strategic models, Big Data, business development, ethics for SBM and other areas.

Please note that whilst our *Strategic Business Management Exam Room Notes* do contain summaries of the financial reporting areas tested in recent SBM examinations, we would recommend that you take this set of *Advanced Level Financial Reporting Exam Room Notes* into your SBM examination (even if you also purchase our *Strategic Business Management Exam Room Notes*) as this will provide the maximum possible coverage of the different FR areas that could be tested.

Our *Strategic Business Management Exam Room Notes* are the only set of Advanced Level Exam Room Notes which are specific to a particular Advanced Level paper – our other 2 sets of Advanced Level Exam Room Notes (*Advanced Level Audit & Assurance Exam Room Notes* and *Advanced Level Financial Reporting Exam Room Notes*) are useful for **both** CR and SBM.

For further information on these resources, please see our website at **www.acasimplified.com**.

How to Use this Book and Revision Advice

Thank you for purchasing this set of *Advanced Level Financial Reporting Exam Room Notes 2019*. We have reviewed and fully updated the 2018 edition of the book in light of the new 2019 Corporate Reporting syllabus including the very extensive syllabus changes in relation to IFRS 9 and IFRS 15.

We have carefully summarised and simplified the complex ACA Financial Reporting syllabus (both Advanced Level and Professional Level) into **77** key topic areas. We have arranged these topics **alphabetically** for ease of reference: we believe that this is a more sensible presentation than organising the topics by Study Manual chapter (particularly as our content is derived from the Study Manuals for **both** Corporate Reporting and the Professional Level paper in Financial Accounting and Reporting!) – using our presentation, you can skip straight to the topic without having to remember which chapter of the Study Manuals (or related notes) to check.

We present a complete **alphabetical list of topics starting on page 15**. If you know what topic you need to check, then use this list to quickly find the correct page. Alternatively, simply flick through the book looking at the headings in the top right of the page to find the topic.

We would emphasise that our notes are merely intended to be memory joggers to be used in the exam – you must also invest some time in learning the relevant principles and practising full questions: you will not pass simply from using this book with no other preparation and you must get some experience of using the book in practice exams so that you understand (1) what information is available in the book and (2) where to find it quickly.

We also strongly recommend that you highlight the points which are important to you – we have tried to prepare full and thorough notes to cover all exam-relevant aspects in each topic but everyone is different and so you will need to work out what is most useful to you personally.

Without undertaking our recommended careful practice and familiarisation using this book before the examination, you will spend too long looking around for information when in the examination you need to be working as quickly as possible and simply using the book as a memory jogger of content that you have learnt well already. **The more you use the book before the examination, the more quickly you will be able to work in the examination itself** – working quickly is absolutely vital for your examination and you must at all costs avoid spending too long looking points up whilst the countdown timer is ticking down on examination day!

Where possible, we include a **suggested mark allocation for a topic** (assuming that the topic is examined in the **FR-focused** CR question: normally Q2 in CR) to give you some guidance as to how much time to spend on a particular topic. The suggested mark allocation is based on our review of past paper markschemes, as well as our judgement and experience, including our experience of teaching the old Business Reporting paper on which Corporate Reporting is heavily based. However, **always use your own judgement to determine the number of marks**, looking firstly at the amount of Exhibit material relating to the issue (the more material, the more marks) and also looking at the other topics tested (these may clearly be worth a large or small number of marks, allowing you to work out the likely mark allocation of the other parts of the question using a balancing approach) before deciding on your mark and time allocation.

For some topics which have not been examined to date we have not included a suggested mark allocation as this would not be based on any hard data and could be misleading. Therefore, the fact that a particular topic does not state a suggested mark allocation is not an error or omission in the book.

Please note that, as indicated, the suggested mark allocation assumes that you are attempting the **FR-focused CR question** (normally Q2 in CR). You should reduce the mark allocation to perhaps 2/3 of the estimate stated when you are attempting the audit-focused or mixed audit & FR questions (normally Q1 and Q3, respectively, in CR) as the markscheme will have to make room for auditing marks – the markscheme is designed to prevent you passing simply because you are very good at only **one** of the technical areas of (1) FR **or** (2) auditing. Therefore, if you are strong at FR please do not try to do too much FR in the audit-focused or mixed audit & FR questions!

We strongly recommend that you use this book in all revision and practice Mock attempts from now on – otherwise you will not learn where to find the necessary information under time pressure.

How Not to Use this Book

Please do not try to use this book in the examination without first spending some time getting used to where to find relevant information. It is not possible simply to turn up on exam day and expect to pass by using this book – rather, you must prepare fully before the examination by practising plenty of questions and reading the Study Manual. This book will simply provide you with **reminders** of content that you should already know – it will not provide you with everything you need to know on a topic that you have not properly studied already.

We have tried to organise the notes in a user-friendly manner, using an alphabetical approach as far as possible. However, there is no substitute for actively using the book during your practice attempts, allowing you to understand and highlight the priority reminder areas for you personally, as this will ensure that you know where to locate the necessary information.

Inline Definition Concept – The Importance of Avoiding a Generic Answer

We have tried to produce a detailed and thorough set of notes which focuses on key definitional and technical issues. This should give you all the gener**al** reminders that you need but in order to prevent your answer therefore becoming gener**ic** in nature it is important that you apply the **general** points to the **specific** data and scenario given. You must definitely avoid a "listing out" approach where you simply copy out the IFRS standards – anyone can copy out material so this is not what the examiners want to see.

Rather than first copying out the IFRS rules and only then going on to refer to the data/Exhibit (or running out of time to properly use the data because you have spent too long writing out the IFRS rules), we strongly recommend that you work the other way around and use what we call "inline definition". This means that you **first identify and quote something relevant from the data/Exhibit** and only then refer to the IFRS rule/definition in the second part of the sentence (but all in the same line of writing). This will prevent you copying out generic content at the start of your answer which you go on to repeat anyway when you apply the rules to the data.

As an example, rather than simply writing out the 3 criteria for a provision to be recognised before then looking at the data, start with the data and state if this indicates whether 1 or more of the criteria are satisfied. For example, you could say that "The conclusion of the legal case creates a 'past obligating event' and the entity's legal team is confident that the figure of £2m is a 'reliable estimate' of a 'probable outflow of economic resources'". This sentence **both defines and applies in the same line** so it is a much more efficient use of time than copying out definitions and only then moving to the application section (in practice, we know that because of this problem many students who have an inefficient writing style often do not even get to the application section in some parts of the answer, leaving them only with some copied out definitional points which will not really score very well).

How to Use this Book and Revision Advice

Forex Consolidation – The Importance of Taking in a Worked Example

We have provided detailed reminder notes on how to consolidate a foreign subsidiary into the group accounts in our section starting on **page 84**. Hopefully these notes will help you understand the process. However, given the complexity of forex consolidation and the fact that this topic has not been tested as an entire question yet in CR, we would strongly recommend that you find a reasonably detailed example of a forex consolidation from a recent past paper or the Question Bank and take an annotated version of your chosen example into the examination with you. Together with the reminders in this book, such a resource should give you a good chance of performing well in this tricky topic which was occasionally the basis of an entire financial reporting question (the equivalent of CR Q2) under the predecessor Business Reporting paper …

In respect of all other topics, we believe that the notes provided here should be sufficient in themselves – however, as advised above, you are strongly recommended to practise a number of questions whilst using this book as this practice will reveal whether you feel you need any additional pro formas or notes. We have tried to be thorough but everyone will have their own preferences in terms of information required, based on their own strengths and weaknesses.

Some General Tips Regarding Revision for the Advanced Level

We strongly recommend that you do as many practice questions as possible from the relevant Study Manual (whether CR or SBM) and do not rely simply on the Question Bank. We know that the instinct of many students is to go straight to the Question Bank but in both CR and SBM we have seen several past paper questions where the content is closer to the example questions within the Study Manual than it is to anything contained in any Question Bank questions. We think it is quite likely that the examiners will have the Study Manual open and in front of them when they are setting questions to ensure that the questions are fair and only cover content within the Study Manual: for this purpose, the Question Bank is less relevant. Whilst we recognise there are a large number of questions in the Study Manual (particularly for CR), we do believe that this will be time well spent.

We strongly recommend that you build some time into your revision plan to review your FAR and A&A notes from these Professional Level papers. We also recommend that you allocate some study time to practise past papers from both of these subjects. This is because a large number of marks at the Advanced Level will be based on brought-forward knowledge rather than the content of the Advanced Level study materials. The examiners frequently comment that the level of brought-forward knowledge is poor (particularly in relation to Groups) so they are likely to continue to test this knowledge and, after all, the Advanced Level is the last opportunity for the examiners to test your professional competence as a Chartered Accountant – you should still be able to explain the IFRS treatment of brought-forward topics, as well as to advise on audit risks and procedures, if you will be soon going on to practise as a Chartered Accountant.

We are aware that many students tend to focus on the new Advanced Level study materials and this is completely understandable because there is a lot to learn and some areas such as forex consolidation and Deferred Tax are quite complicated. However, you should be aware that in many Advanced Level papers **over half of the marks available are actually for brought-forward topics**. For this reason, we have reviewed the FAR syllabus in detail and have also analysed FAR past papers and ICAEW Mocks when preparing this set of *Advanced Level Financial Reporting Exam Room Notes 2019*. Hopefully our notes will give you some useful reminders but obviously it will be best if you have also revised your brought-forward knowledge yourself.

In addition to this set of *Advanced Level Financial Reporting Exam Room Notes 2019*, we do have a number of other resources available to help you with the Advanced Level:

How to Use this Book and Revision Advice

Advanced Level Audit & Assurance Q&A 2019 – hundreds of short form practice questions to learn the Audit & Assurance syllabus in an active way

Advanced Level Financial Reporting Q&A 2019 – hundreds of short form practice questions to learn the Financial Reporting syllabus in an active way

Advanced Level Audit & Assurance Exam Room Notes 2019 – very similar to this book but relating to the important area of audit risks & procedures and also specialist assurance topics such as Corporate Governance, Internal Audit, ISAE 3400, and so on

Strategic Business Management Exam Room Notes 2019 – again very similar to this book but covering all key SBM numerical and narrative areas

Smashing Strategic Business Management 2019 – our student-focused and practical guide to planning and revising for the SBM examination, including explanation of our unique MAP planning strategy, revision of key assurance, business strategy and financial management areas and detailed discussion of writing style and ethics for SBM.

Please see our website at **www.acasimplified.com** for further details on the above texts.

As a large number of Advanced Level marks will be available for brought-forward knowledge (see discussion above), you may also be interested in our set of Professional Level materials – to assist with your revision, we would particularly recommend our *Audit & Assurance Q&A 2019* and *Financial Accounting & Reporting Q&A 2019* for CR and our *Business Strategy Q&A 2019* and *Financial Management Q&A 2019* for SBM.

Updates Within the 2019 Advanced Level Financial Reporting Syllabus

Unlike in many recent prior years, unfortunately the updates to create the 2019 syllabus for the financial reporting elements of the Advanced Level are very significant indeed, particularly in relation to financial instruments (where IFRS 9 is now the main examinable standard) and revenue (where IFRS 15 is now the main examinable standard). ICAEW have created entirely new chapters of content and related practice questions on IFRS 9 and IFRS 15 for the 2019 editions of the Corporate Reporting and Strategic Business Management Study Manuals. We have therefore had to spend a lot more time than usual updating our Advanced Level materials and if you took the Advanced Level examinations in 2018 or earlier, you too will unfortunately have to do quite a lot of work to update your knowledge. Please also be careful if you use any ICAEW resources such as Mock exams for 2018 or earlier years as these will now be out of date.

ICAEW have fully updated the 2019 editions of the Corporate Reporting and Strategic Business Management Question Banks (including any past papers incorporated into the Question Banks) so these resources will accordingly be more important than in prior years when all ICAEW Mocks and past papers related to the same financial instruments (IAS 39) and revenue (IAS 18) rules.

At the same time, it is important to recognise that the changes in relation to financial reporting areas other than revenue and financial instruments are relatively minor. This is good news if you have taken the examinations in 2018 or earlier as you can therefore focus on IFRS 9 and IFRS 15 in terms of knowledge updates.

We have set out below the main changes that we have identified in the 2019 edition of the Corporate Reporting Study Manual. As the Strategic Business Management Study Manual contains condensed versions of the same financial reporting rules set out in the Corporate Reporting Study Manual, we have only analysed the changes in the Corporate Reporting Study Manual below. (Accordingly, all references to the "Study Manual" and all page references in the remainder of this sub-section are to the 2019 edition of the Corporate Reporting Study Manual).

How to Use this Book and Revision Advice

A. Revised Conceptual Framework (March 2018)

The 2019 edition of the Study Manual adds some narrative content on the revised Conceptual Framework dated March 2018. Do not panic! The revised Conceptual Framework is not yet fully examinable but candidates are required to have some awareness of the main contents of the revised version. See page 70 of the Study Manual for relevant content. Further content can also be found on page 93 which also looks at how the Conceptual Framework project is being taken into account for disclosure and materiality purposes.

B. IFRS 9 as the main examinable standard on financial instruments

With effect from the 2019 Advanced Level syllabus, IFRS 9 replaces IAS 39 as the main examinable standard on financial instruments. IAS 39 rules remain relevant in relation to hedge accounting (entities currently have a choice whether to apply IFRS 9 or IAS 39 rules on hedge accounting) but in respect of all other financial instruments areas, the Study Manual replaces references to IAS 39 with references to IFRS 9. Please therefore now forget about the IAS 39 categories of Available for Sale (AFS), Loans and Receivables (L&R) and Held to Maturity (HTM) as these are no longer relevant: relatedly, please watch out for any practice questions or notes that you may already have which refer to these concepts as such resources should no longer be used.

The 2019 Study Manual makes numerous minor changes to replace references to IAS 39 with references to IFRS 9. Sometimes these are quite literally simply just a direct replacement of the words "IAS 39" with the words "IFRS 9" whilst on other occasions the change of course involves a more substantive adjustment. There are too many of these changes scattered throughout the Study Manual for us to list out here.

Instead, we would recommend that you concentrate your efforts on reviewing chapter 16 and chapter 17 of the 2019 edition of the Study Manual as these chapters have been very extensively revised for the new IFRS 9 rules. (Fortunately, chapter 15 of the Study Manual, which focuses on IAS 32, has hardly been changed for 2019 as IAS 32 has not been amended by IFRS 9 and remains a relevant standard in relation to financial instruments.) A large number of useful practice questions have been newly introduced by the examiners so please do familiarise yourself with these examples because we do find that the examiners rely quite heavily on Study Manual examples when introducing a new topic area into the real examinations for the first time. Such examples have been designed with an explicit focus on the relevant new standard and so may be a superior form of preparation to Question Bank questions where the examiners have had to "patch up" prior questions to amend the content for IFRS 9 – whilst such "patched up" questions are of course also useful and indeed form the basis of the notes on IFRS 9 and IFRS 15 provided in this set of *Exam Room Notes* (see page 12 for further explanation of our approach here), this kind of question was never designed from the ground up to test the unique aspects of IFRS 9 rules (rather, they were designed to emphasise IAS 39 rules) so the Question Bank question may well leave very important aspects of IFRS 9 untested whereas the Study Manual questions will not suffer from this potential weakness as a form of preparation (whilst of course not necessarily being full exam-standard questions themselves).

C. IFRS 15 as the main examinable standard on revenue

Chapter 10 of the Study Manual has been rewritten from scratch by the examiners to reflect the fact that IFRS 15 is now the main examinable standard. A number of very useful practice examples have been added to the new chapter 10. As advised in relation to financial instruments above, please do familiarise yourself with these new Study Manual examples (rather than just "hitting the Question Bank") because we do think that there is a strong likelihood that the examiners will stick closely to the Study Manual examples when drafting entirely new questions on IFRS 15 (and IFRS 9) – whilst the 2019 edition of the Question Bank has been updated for the new rules, such updates amount to a "patching up" of questions that were originally drafted under the old set of rules and which were therefore never designed to test the key and unique features of IFRS 15 (and IFRS 9). Therefore, the Study Manual practice questions are, in our view, a very important resource this year.

However, in line with our general approach in this book of relying as much as possible on example answers to derive our notes (rather than attempting simply to summarise the Study Manual content), we have primarily relied on the amended past paper and Question Bank examples contained in the 2019 edition of the Corporate Reporting Question Bank (see page 12 for further explanation of our approach here).

D. IFRS 17

The 2019 edition of the Study Manual slightly amends the discussion of IFRS 17 on pages 669 and 670. Although we do not expect the incoming standard IFRS 17 to be a particularly examinable standard (it relates to insurance contracts, which are obviously a rather niche area of financial reporting on which it may be difficult to set a wide-ranging question which is fair to candidates), with the move of IFRS 9 and IFRS 15 into the category of fully examinable standards, there is an accordingly reduced range of "incoming" standards on which the examiners can draw if they want to award marks to candidates who can add value to their answers by explaining to the client how future reporting periods could be impacted by incoming rules changes.

E. IFRS 16

The 2019 edition of the Study Manual makes some changes in the discussion of IFRS 16, a future incoming standard which was nevertheless tested in both 2018 Corporate Reporting past papers. See page 753, page 756, page 757 and page 764 in particular.

As discussed in relation to IFRS 17 above, with the move of IFRS 9 and IFRS 15 into the category of fully examinable standards, there is an accordingly reduced range of "incoming" standards on which the examiners can draw, potentially making IFRS 16 more examinable (particularly given that with its focus on leases, a known favourite area of the examiners, IFRS 16 would be easier to integrate into an interesting examination question than a more "niche" standard such as IFRS 17). Having said this, as already noted above, IFRS 16 was already tested in both 2018 Corporate Reporting past papers and it surely cannot come up on every paper!

F. Pensions and Share-based payment: minor narrative additions

Pensions and share-based payment have, for some years now, been staple and unchanging "favourites" of candidates i.e. relatively straightforward areas based on a formulaic numerical approach and where the examiners cannot pull too many "tricks" from a narrative point of view.

Some minor narrative points have been added in relation to pensions on page 986 of the Study Manual and in relation to share-based payment on page 1010 of the Study Manual. Once again, do not panic! It does not appear that these changes have made any significant difference to the content set out in the remainder of chapters 18 and 19, respectively, so these areas can remain "favourites" (and not just for students!). We simply wanted to point out these small additions as they represent the first changes on these "staple" topics for several years.

G. Deferred Tax

As you are hopefully already aware, Deferred Tax is definitely a favourite area for the examiners (although this time perhaps not necessarily for students …): the topic of Deferred Tax has appeared on most Corporate Reporting past papers to date.

Therefore, it is worth making yourself familiar with some minor additions to the 2019 edition of the Corporate Reporting Study Manual on page 1263 (addition of a tabular explanation of Deferred Tax principles), page 1266 (new summary diagram on Deferred Tax), page 1267 (discussion of Deferred Tax on intangible assets) and page 1286 (addition of a short section on general principles of Deferred Tax in a group scenario).

How to Use this Book and Revision Advice

Overall, as you can see, with the exception of the changes in relation to IFRS 9 and IFRS 15, the changes for the 2019 syllabus are relatively minor. Even so, we hope that you will take the opportunity to review all of the above key changes to ensure that you are as well-prepared as possible for the examination.

Sources Used

To develop this book, we have reviewed the following sources of key points which the examiners want to see in your answers:

> CR past papers (covering the period from launch of the CR paper in July 2014 to the latest available model answers for the November 2018 examination)

> CR ICAEW Mocks (2 papers per sitting covering the period from launch of the CR paper in July 2014 to the latest available model answers for the November 2018 Mocks)

> CR ICAEW Question Bank 2019 (covering all questions in the Question Bank)

> FAR past papers (covering the period from launch of the FAR paper in September 2013 to the latest available model answers for the December 2018 examination)

> FAR ICAEW Mocks (2 papers per sitting covering the period from launch of the FAR paper in September 2013 to the latest available model answers for the December 2018 Mocks)

We have reviewed FAR materials because the examiners will most certainly test brought-forward Professional Level knowledge at the Advanced Level – please do not fall into the classic mistake of concentrating too much on Advanced Level knowledge: **most of the marks for financial reporting in a typical CR paper will actually be based on brought-forward topics**. (Please see our discussion above for some general tips and discussion regarding this point.)

In cases where a topic has not been examined to date but has a substantial Study Manual section dedicated to it (for example, Agriculture or Regulatory Deferral Accounts) we have summarised the relevant Study Manual section as there is no past paper or ICAEW Mock content to consider. **However, this is very much the exception and we have, wherever possible, relied on past paper, ICAEW Mock or Question Bank model answers in order to ensure that we have focused on points that are more likely to rewarded.**

This means that our notes on IFRS 9 and IFRS 15 in this book are relatively short compared to the very detailed technical discussion in the relevant chapters of the 2019 edition of the Corporate Reporting Study Manual. Whilst we have still created several pages on a wide range of areas relating to these standards, both IFRS 9 and IFRS 15 have very long Study Manual chapter content and we have obviously not been able to summarise all eventualities for the purposes of this book.

Rather than trying to summarise the new Study Manual content on these areas, we have taken the decision to focus on summarising the available model answers on these topics (as with all other topics) but because these 2 new IFRS standards are only fully examinable from 2019 onwards we do not have the same existing bank of example questions (such as prior year ICAEW Mocks or FAR past papers) that we have for other topics. This necessarily means that our notes may appear to be quite short relative to the content in the Study Manual on these standards, given their complexity.

We have taken the decision to concentrate on the relatively narrow set of available IFRS 9 and IFRS 15 model answers on the basis that if we tried to summarise the hugely complex Study Manual chapters on these areas then we would end up with unmanageably long sets of notes which would not be of use to students under time pressure in the examination (and therefore would not be helpful as "exam room notes",

How to Use this Book and Revision Advice

defeating the purpose of this book). Hopefully we will have captured the more examinable areas of these topics by following the same approach used in relation to all other topics in this book i.e. focusing on model answers as our primary source.

Disclaimers

This book has been developed by reviewing official ICAEW materials such as the Study Manual, Question Bank, past papers and Mocks. In preparing the book, we have assumed that these ICAEW materials are correct unless a relevant errata sheet has been issued by ICAEW. Given the time constraints to produce the book, we have not checked every single technical point back to the underlying IFRS rules and have instead **assumed that the ICAEW materials are correct**. We cannot be held responsible for any errors in the underlying ICAEW material which had not been notified to tutor companies before the time of finalisation of the script of this book (March 2019).

We have developed this set of *Advanced Level Financial Reporting Exam Room Notes 2019* by working backwards from common themes in model answers to identify the core areas that you need to cover to ensure a passing grade – our aim has not been to summarise every page of the relevant Study Manuals (either Professional or Advanced Level) nor to try to cover every possible way in which topics **could** be tested: if we tried to do this, we would end up with a book the same length as the Study Manuals and therefore not suitable as a **quick reference resource** in the examination. Our aim has been to create an "exam-focused" text i.e. one that responds to the most commonly tested areas and highlights the most common student errors when attempting to answer these areas rather than a text which is designed as any kind of substitute for proper study of the Study Manual. **Many of the changes made to create the 2019 syllabus appear to us to be highly technical in nature and only relevant in very specific scenarios so we have not added every additional 2019 syllabus point into this book. Please see our comments regarding IFRS 9 and IFRS 15 in particular in the previous section above.**

We have also concentrated primarily on including the points **contained in model answers** as sometimes valid points contained in the Study Manuals do not appear to be given credit and therefore you would be wasting time to include these points (even if they are completely correct from a technical point of view). No book of the type we have tried to write here can cover every possible matter that could be tested from a combination of 2 different ACA papers (FAR and CR) and there is a **very significant risk** of running out of time if you go into matters in too much detail so we have purposefully not tried to cover everything.

In any examination, you will need to apply your general understanding to the specific scenario set and we cannot anticipate exactly what will be required. Therefore, we do not make any claim that this book covers all potential examination points – it has instead been designed to help you with the **more commonly assessed points**. We therefore cannot accept any complaints that the book did not cover every single issue tested in your own particular examination as the book is instead designed to help you ensure a good performance in the **more commonly-tested areas** which should almost certainly constitute more than enough marks to obtain a passing grade in any CR examination.

Finally, please note that all examiners' reports for the Advanced Level examinations complain about candidates using "**generic**" points in their answers – this is a particular problem at the Advanced Level because students are able to refer extensively to their own notes in these "open book" examinations and so there is a tendency for students to list out too much content from those notes, either because the information in their notes is easily available and definitely correct or because students do not quite know how to answer the specific examination scenario and therefore resort to the "comfort blanket" of copying out as much as possible from their notes in the hope of scoring some form of credit. The points that we have included in these notes are simply meant to **remind** you of technical content that you should already know and we **very strongly recommend against simply copying out the points made in this book** – many of these may not be relevant to your specific question and you must in any case show the examiner that you have responded to the specific scenario information given in your question – **anyone can copy out notes and you will not be rewarded for doing so**.

Thank you for reading these disclaimers and we hope this section has made it clearer to you how the book should (and should not) be used.

A Reminder About Copyright

Please do not photocopy or otherwise distribute this book, either in whole or part. Copyright theft is a crime and we will pursue individuals who infringe our copyright. Copyright theft is a clear breach of professional ethics and may therefore be reported to ICAEW.

We have put a considerable amount of time and effort into developing innovative materials which we genuinely feel will give you an edge in the exams. We would be grateful if you would respect these efforts by not copying this text.

Errors

All content in this book has been carefully written and checked. We have made every effort to ensure that there are no errors.

If you believe you have discovered an error (other than formatting or spelling), please do notify us as soon as possible using the contact information provided on the ACA Simplified website. We will then investigate the matter for you. If something just does not seem to make sense, please do not suffer in silence – get in touch.

Feedback

We hope that you will find this set of *Advanced Level Financial Reporting Exam Room Notes 2019* helps your revision, in particular by making it as time-efficient as possible.

We wish you all the best in the exam and would be very pleased to hear how you got on. We would also be grateful to hear your feedback on this book. We are keen to provide the best quality revision materials but can only do so with your feedback.

Please use the contact information provided on the ACA Simplified website if you would like to get in touch.

Thanks again for your purchase and good luck with your examinations!

List of Acronyms

CSFP	Consolidated Statement of Financial Position
CSoCIE	Consolidated Statement of Changes in Equity
CSPL	Consolidated Statement of Profit or Loss
NCI	Non-Controlling Interest
P&L	Profit or Loss account
SCF	Statement of Cash Flows
SFP	Statement of Financial Position
SoCIE	Statement of Changes in Equity

Note – although some ICAEW materials now use the term "profit **or** loss" rather than the term "profit **and** loss", we have left in place our "P&L" acronym in the interests of preserving consistency and therefore reducing the chances of causing confusion by changing only some of our "P&L" references. You will not lose marks in the examination if you use the terms "profit **and** loss" or "P&L": the marks will be given for correctly stating whether the issue is appropriately recognised in the P&L or, alternatively, OCI so you will be awarded the marks if you get this fundamental issue correct: the precise terminology used will not affect whether credit is given.

Table of Contents

	Page
Other ACA Simplified Resources for CR and SBM (and a discount!)	3
How to Use This Book and Revision Advice	5
List of Acronyms	14
General Tips for Answering CR Questions	18
Accounting Policies, Changes in Accounting Estimates and Errors	21
Agriculture	23
Assets Held for Sale and Discontinued operations	25
Borrowing costs	28
Cash Flow Statement – Example	30
Consolidated Statement of Changes in Equity (CSoCIE)	32
Customer loyalty programmes	33
Deferred tax	34
DEPS	40
Derivatives and Embedded Derivatives	43
Distributable Profits	46
EPS	48
Ethics	50
Events After the Reporting Period	58
Fair Value – IFRS 13	60
Financial instruments – convertible bonds	62
Financial instruments – IFRS 9	63
Financial instruments – impairment – IFRS 9	68
Forex translation – single entity accounts	71
Going Concern	73
Government Grants	74
Groups – acquisitions	77
Groups – associates	79
Groups – associate to subsidiary	80
Groups – disposal of a subsidiary	82

Table of Contents

	Page
Groups – forex consolidation	84
Groups – goodwill calculation	89
Groups – impairment and NCI	92
Groups – step acquisition	93
Groups – step disposal	95
Groups – subsidiary	98
Groups – subsidiary to associate	99
Groups – subsidiary to subsidiary	100
Hedge accounting – cash flow hedge	101
Hedge accounting – fair value hedge	104
Hedge accounting – general	106
Hedge accounting – hedge of a net investment	107
Hedge accounting – IFRS 9 detailed rules	109
Hedge accounting – IFRS 9 versus IAS 39	113
Holiday pay accrual	115
Impairment	116
Impairment – CGU	117
Insurance Contracts	119
Intangibles	122
Interim Financial Reporting	125
Inventories	128
Investment Property	129
Joint Arrangements	134
Leases – dealer/manufacturer	136
Leases – finance leases	137
Leases – IFRS 16	140
Leases – lease incentives	143
Leases – operating leases	144
Mineral Resources	145
Onerous Contracts	147
Operating Segments	148

Table of Contents

	Page
Pension schemes – narrative on different types	150
Pension schemes – pro formas and disclosures	151
Performance review – tips	155
Performance review – ratios	157
Provisions	160
Regulatory Deferral Accounts	162
Related Party Transactions	163
Research & Development	166
Revenue Recognition – IFRS 15	168
Rights Issue	173
Sale and Finance Leaseback	175
Sale and Operating Leaseback	176
Sale and Repurchase	178
Share-based payment – cash-settled	179
Share-based payment – equity-settled	180
Share-based payment – payment for goods and services	184
Share-based payment – Share Appreciation Rights	185
Share-based payment – share options – summary of treatment	186
Social and environmental reporting	188
Staff bonuses	189
Treasury shares	190

General Tips for Answering CR Questions

Although this set of *Exam Room Notes* is relevant to both the Corporate Reporting and Strategic Business Management examinations, we include in this section some examination technique tips which are specific to your answering style in CR questions since CR will obviously include more extensive testing of financial reporting content than SBM.

Use the scenario!

Anyone can copy out standards from notes or the IFRS book – only a good candidate can apply their knowledge to the **unique aspects of the scenario set**.

Make sure your answer is scenario-specific by referring extensively to key **facts and figures** stated in the scenario Exhibits – avoid a "**listing out**" approach.

Inline definition

Relatedly, rather than copying out a standard at the start of the question, try to start your sentences with key facts and figures from the scenario and only **then** mention the relevant IFRS rules **as you go along** (in the **second part** of each sentence).

This way you will show that you know the rules but you will be guaranteeing that you are **also** using the **data** because you are starting your points with Exhibit information which could not have been pre-prepared.

Journals – check what you are being asked to do (journals from scratch or adjusting journals)

Always read the question wording carefully to check whether you need to incrementally **adjust** any entries **already made** or whether the journal is required **from scratch** (i.e. no entry at all has been made by the client) – the examiners have stated that students often assume that no entries have been made but in practice it is very common to require only a **correcting** journal to what the client has already mistakenly done.

Note that what the client accountant has already done will **very often be wrong** …

Do not forget the NCI (and do not be afraid of him!)

For some reason we find that students are very reluctant to mention the impact of their adjustments/treatment on the NCI in group questions. This is simply a matter of multiplying the adjustment/treatment by a percentage figure (reflecting the NCI holding) so is a very easy way of generating some more marks. The marking will work on a follow through basis so you can still get all the NCI marks even if your approach to the underlying adjustment/rule itself is wrong.

So as soon as you see that you are attempting a group scenario then make a note somewhere to mention the NCI impact.

General Tips for Answering CR Questions

Ratios – do not go nuts!

If you enjoy the numbers side of accounting, do not go too crazy with the number of performance ratios and metrics which you calculate – you could calculate figures all day but the point is to state the **key points** in a short space of time.

The ICAEW Corporate Reporting Question Bank contains several questions with 25+ marks for performance review work – note that the real exam papers have thus far allocated **far fewer marks** for performance review as there are also other elements of the question to address.

Therefore do not spend too long on the performance review just because it is relatively straightforward.

Think which question you are attempting

If you are doing the FR-heavy question (generally Q2 in the recent CR examinations) then you will need to go into reasonable **depth** and look at **both** the numbers and narrative aspects to score well. However, if you are attacking exactly the same topic in the other questions (audit-focused and mixed audit & FR) then bear in mind that the number of marks available for any given Financial Reporting topic will be **lower**. Hence just be careful to make your answer a little shorter as otherwise you will spend too long on an issue that is necessarily worth fewer marks simply because it is not being tested in the FR-heavy question.

It is for this reason that our mark allocation estimates are based on assuming that the topic is being tested in an FR-heavy question – ensure that you reduce your mark estimate and related time allocation accordingly if you are not attempting the FR-heavy question.

Am I secretly not very good at Audit?

If you are not an auditor in your day to day work then please ensure that you do write enough for the audit sections of the paper – it is not possible to pass the exam just from great FR work so do not try to hide behind this ability. You must confront your weaker skill and allow enough time to get a good number of audit marks or you will not get the total number of marks needed.

Do not go straight for the calculations

There are indeed specific marks for getting the calculations correct – but the number of marks is nowhere near as many as you may expect. In fact, there will be a lot of marks (and often the **majority** of the marks available) for narrative explanation of the principles and use of the scenario data. Do not neglect these marks by spending too long on the calculations.

Equally, remember that the marking is done on a full follow-through approach so even if your figures are wrong but are correctly discussed then you can still pick up a good number of marks … but only if you leave yourself enough time for writing by not spending too long on the calculations.

Adjustments to the financial statements/Schedule of Uncorrected Misstatements

Often the question will ask you either to process your suggested changes and show how the financial statements would be affected or, in an audit question, to produce a Schedule of Uncorrected Misstatements that shows a 4 column presentation of the Dr and Cr adjustments needed regarding both the Income Statement and the Statement of Financial Position.

These adjustments/schedules are marked on a full follow through approach so you have a chance of scoring all the marks if you simply attempt the section and pull through your figures. There tend to be around 6 marks for doing so, which is relatively generous when everything is based on a follow through approach so **please leave enough time to give this section a good attempt**.

You may wish to set up the adjustments/schedule and add points as you go along when answering the other parts of the question, rather than leaving this as a separate task – at least this way you will definitely start getting **some** of the marks from the adjustments/schedule part of the markscheme whereas if you do not make a start on this part of the answer until you have first dealt with all the issues then there is a chance you might never get started and all those easy, follow through marks will be lost instantly …

Audit procedures – put lots in! And don't just say "Check payables" or similar!

The examiners want to see a large number of procedures mentioned, across a range of risk areas – we would aim for at least 4 different tests per risk area and try to mix these tests up so that you are not just recycling the same test each time.

We do not recommend use of the term "check" in relation to any audit tests – obviously auditing involves the "checking" of information so do not expect any marks to be available for stating such a truism. Additionally, the point of the marks for audit tests and procedures is to spell out exactly **how** the auditor will check information so simply saying "check" does not really answer the question at all.

Accounting Policies, Changes in Accounting Estimates and Errors

The rules here are governed by IAS 8

Accounting policies should be applied consistently for similar transactions, events and conditions

Changes in accounting policy should be rare and should only be made if required by an IFRS or if the change will result in the provision of more reliable and relevant information about the effect of transactions, events or conditions on the entity's position, performance or cash flows

Events which do not constitute a change in accounting policy

Adopting an accounting policy for a **new type** of transaction or event not dealt with previously by the entity

Adopting a **new** accounting policy for a transaction or event which has **not occurred in the past** or which was not material

A decision to adopt a policy of **revaluation** under IAS 16 is not treated as a change of accounting policy under IAS 8

Changes in accounting policy

Such a change must be applied **retrospectively** by adjusting the opening balance of retained earnings

Comparative information should be **restated** unless it is **impracticable** to do so – all comparative information is restated as if the new policy had **always been in force**

In the case of voluntary changes, the nature of the change, reasons for the change (why more reliable and relevant), amount of adjustments and the fact that comparative information has been restated (or that it is impracticable to do so) should be disclosed

Changes in accounting estimates

Such changes must be recognised **prospectively** only

These changes result from new information or new developments and are not corrections of errors

Examples – bad debt (receivables) allowances, useful lives of depreciable assets, adjustments for obsolescence of inventory

Where a change in accounting estimate has a **material** effect in the current period there should be **disclosure** of the **nature** of the change in the accounting estimate and the amount of change (or disclosure of the fact that it is impractical to estimate this)

Cases of doubt

If there is **doubt** as to which type of change has occurred (change in accounting policy or change in accounting estimate), IAS 8 requires the change to be treated as a change in accounting **estimate**

Accounting Policies, Changes in Accounting Estimates and Errors

Prior period errors

If **immaterial**, these can be corrected through net profit or loss for the **current** period

If **material**, prior period errors should be corrected **retrospectively** – this means there must be recognition, measurement and disclosure of amounts as if the prior period error had never occurred (restating the comparative amounts or, if that is not possible, the opening balances for the earliest prior period presented)

There should be disclosure of the nature of the prior period error, the amount of the correction for each financial statement line item affected, the amount of the correction at the start of the earliest prior period presented and, if retrospective restatement is impracticable, the circumstances which have caused this impracticability and a description of how and from when the error has been corrected

Agriculture

IAS 41 applies permanently to **biological** assets – however, it only applies to **agricultural produce** up to the point of harvest (after this point IAS 2 *Inventories* applies)

Characteristics of agricultural activities

Capacity to change – a seed grows into a tree; a lamb grows into a sheep

Management of change – reliant on some form of management input for survival

Measurement of change – quality and quantity can both change

Note – ocean fishing is not an agricultural activity as there is no management intervention for the fish to grow: this just happens naturally

Bearer biological assets

These are plant-based biological assets such as grape vines, rubber trees and oil palms

These plants grow crops over several periods and are not themselves consumed – when they are no longer productive they are usually scrapped

These plants should be accounted for under IAS 16 (including the option to use the revaluation model) as they are not directly subject to IAS 41 because they do not have a fair value **themselves** – rather the value is in what they **produce**

The produce of these assets continues to be recognised under IAS 41

Recognition of biological or agricultural assets

Entity **controls** the asset as a result of past events

Probable flow of future economic **benefits** to the entity

FV or cost can be **measured reliably**

Measurement of biological assets

Measure at FV less estimated CTS

CTS do not include any costs to get the product to market such as transport – these should instead be deducted when arriving at FV

> CTS could include auctioneer's commission, government levies, broker commission, transfer taxes and duties

FV should be based on an active quoted market price or if this does not exist then it should be based on a similar recent transaction, similar market prices or sector benchmarks

If FV cannot be determined then recognise at cost less accumulated depreciation and impairment cost – FV should then be used as soon as reliable measurement can be made

Agriculture

Once FV has been used, it is not possible to revert to cost

Measurement of agricultural produce

Measure at FV less estimated costs to sell at the point of harvest

Subsequent measurement is then made by reference to IAS 2

Grouping of assets

It is permissible to group similar assets together if they have consistent attributes throughout the group

If the assets are physically attached to the land then deduct the FV of the land element from the combined FV – land is dealt with under IAS 16 or IAS 40

Gains or losses

Report these directly in profit or loss as they arise

Gains may arise on recognition of a biological asset e.g. birth of a calf

Gains may arise on harvesting as the harvested crop may be worth more than an unharvested crop

Example

An entity owns 10 animals with an average age of 4 years. Halfway through the year it purchases a 4.5 year old animal. FV less estimated CTS were £100 at the start of the year, £120 for a 4.5 year old animal and £140 for a 5 year old animal

Opening value (10 x £100)	1,000
Purchased	120
Change in FV (balancing figure)	**420**
Closing value (11 x £140)	1,540

Disclosures

The entity is encouraged to disclose separately the amount of change in FV less estimated CTS arising from physical changes and price changes

If it is not possible to apply FV and cost is used instead, an explanation should be provided of why it was not possible to establish FV

A full reconciliation of movements in the net cost should be presented with an explanation of the depreciation rate and method used

Assets Held for Sale and Discontinued operations

Suggested mark allocation in an FR question (CR Q2): 5 marks

Key Tips

AHFS and discontinued operations are often both applied to the same scenario – this is often because the entity is classifying an asset as AHFS as a result of ceasing operations in a certain area, which could lead to a discontinued operation

Do not forget to also consider the **discontinued operations** element – many students spot the **AHFS** aspect but not the **discontinued operations** aspects

Linkages – also consider impairment (IAS 36) and provisions (IAS 37)

AHFS criteria

Available for immediate sale in its present condition

Sale highly probable as evidenced by

- active marketing at a price reasonable in relation to the item's fair value
- changes to the plan for sale are unlikely
- management is committed to the sale
- active programme to locate a buyer
- sale expected to be completed within 1 year from the date of classification (unless delayed by events or circumstances beyond the entity's control, provided that there is sufficient evidence that the entity is still committed to sell the asset)

If the criteria are met only **after** the reporting date, there should be full **disclosure** in the notes to the financial statements (but the asset should not be treated as AHFS in the current accounting period)

Always consider impairment in AHFS questions

Consider **impairment**, especially if the asset is being sold due to a change in business or market conditions

In other cases, the asset may not meet the AHFS criteria but the change in business situation could mean that the asset is still impaired e.g. if the plant has become "surplus to requirements"

- A normal IAS 36 impairment test would then have to be carried out (compare FV less CTS with value in use) – if "surplus to requirements" then value in use will not exceed FV less CTS (because there is no ongoing business value to be obtained from "surplus" equipment) so FV less CTS can be used as the relevant comparator figure

Assets Held for Sale and Discontinued operations

AHFS Treatment – overview

Immediately before classification as held for sale, measure in accordance with the applicable IFRS – therefore an asset held under the IAS 16 revaluation model must be revalued to fair value immediately before any classification as AHFS with the gain or loss treated in the standard way under IAS 16

On classification as AHFS, measure the asset at the **lower** of (1) its carrying amount and (2) FV less costs to sell (impairment test but not under IAS 36 i.e. no need to calculate the recoverable amount)

> If the revaluation model is used, the asset should be revalued under that model before being classified as AHFS (ignoring the costs to sell for this purpose: only look at FV) but if the cost model is used there should NOT be a revaluation to FV (just a write down to FV less CTS, if lower than carrying amount i.e. no revaluation upwards is possible under the cost model) [see also below]

Charge any impairment loss to profit or loss – in the case of an asset held under the IAS 16 revaluation model, costs to sell are treated as an impairment loss (see below)

Cease depreciation or amortisation

Any subsequent changes in FV less CTS are recognised as a further impairment loss or reversal of an impairment loss – however, reversals cannot exceed cumulative impairment losses to date

Once classified as AHFS the costs to sell should be recognised as part of profit or loss for the period

Reclassify the item as a current asset as its value is expected to be realised within the next 12 months

IFRS 5 measurement principles – irrelevance of the recoverable amount

When classified as held for sale, an asset should be measured within current assets at the lower of (1) the carrying amount and (2) fair value – for these purposes, fair value is defined as fair value less costs to sell as there is no requirement to follow the definition in IAS 36 to determine the recoverable amount

Asset under the revaluation model meets the AHFS criteria

First apply the standard IAS 16 approach so revalue the asset to FV (ignoring the costs to sell here) and adjust the revaluation surplus for the gain or loss as required following the normal IAS 16 approach (so any excess loss above the amount in the revaluation surplus is expensed immediately the P&L)

Then apply the usual AHFS rule of setting the AHFS value to be the lower of carrying amount (FV in this case due to the revaluation that has just been put through) and FV less costs to sell – as we have just revalued the asset to FV then the effect in practice must be that the costs to sell are immediately recognised in profit or loss as an impairment loss and the AHFS value of the asset must be FV less costs to sell

Abandonment of non-current assets

Note that the requirements of IFRS 5 relate to assets classified as AHFS because their carrying amounts will be recovered principally through a **sale transaction**

IFRS 5 does **not** apply to assets that will not be **sold** (e.g. scrapped)

Assets Held for Sale and Discontinued operations

Leave such assets in their existing non-current asset category, continue to recognise depreciation and recognise any profit or loss on abandonment at the time of abandonment rather than at the earlier time of the decision to abandon them

IAS 16, rather than IFRS 5, will apply in this case

Discontinued operations

Separate disclosure in the P&L and OCI of a "discontinued operation" is required when a company discontinues a "component" of its activities

> A "discontinued operation" is a separate major line of business or geographical area of operations, part of a single co-ordinated plan to dispose of the same or a subsidiary acquired exclusively with a view to resale

> A "component" should be a cash generating unit, meaning that it comprises operations and cash flows that can be clearly distinguished operationally, and for financial reporting purposes, from the rest of the entity

A single amount in the P&L containing the post-tax profit or loss of discontinued operations and post-tax gain recognised on the measurement to FV less CTS on related assets should be disclosed – this should then be split into revenue, expenses and pre-tax profit or loss, related income tax expense, gain on re-measurement and its related income tax expense

In the Statement of Cash Flows there should be disclosure of the net cash flows attributable to operating, investing and financing activities of discontinued operations

Withdrawal from a particular market or product area could qualify under IFRS 5 but some judgement will be required, particularly if the entity continues to undertake a similar activity in another part of the business or online

Are the operations discontinued?

To be presented as discontinued, the sale of shares in a subsidiary needs to be part of a single coordinated plan to withdraw from a major business line (unless the subsidiary was acquired exclusively with a view to resale: see above)

If there are continuing commercial links between the previous parent company and previous subsidiary company then there may not necessarily be a discontinued operation and the results of the previous subsidiary company should be consolidated into the group accounts as continuing operations through to the date of sale

Motives of Management points

Look out for any incentive for management to treat the operations as "discontinued" in the hope of separately disclosing losses to downplay the significance of those losses by achieving a corresponding improvement in performance from (what management claims are) "continuing" operations

Borrowing costs

Suggested mark allocation in an FR question (CR Q2): 4 marks

Definition

Borrowing costs are defined as **interest and other costs** that an entity incurs in connection with the borrowing of funds in relation to a **qualifying asset** (an asset that necessarily takes a **substantial period** of time to get ready for its intended use or sale)

Only borrowing costs that are **directly attributable** to the acquisition, construction or production of the qualifying asset should be capitalised

Ideally use the interest rate on a loan **specifically taken out** for the purpose of building the asset but a **weighted average cost** is permissible if funded from general borrowing (excluding any borrowings from this calculation if they were taken out to finance a different specific purpose or building)

Qualifying asset

A qualifying asset is an asset that takes a **substantial period of time** to get ready for its intended use or sale

An entity is not required to apply IAS 23 to borrowing costs directly attributable to the acquisition, construction or development of assets which on initial recognition are measured at FV or inventories that are manufactured in large quantities on a repetitive basis even if these take a substantial period of time to get ready for use or sale

Costs to capitalise

Interest expense calculated using the Effective Interest Rate as per IFRS 9

Finance charges in respect of finance leases

However, costs should only relate to borrowing which would have been avoided if the expenditure on the qualifying asset had not been made

If financed out of specific borrowing, use the interest rate applicable to that borrowing

If financed out of general borrowing then use the weighted average cost of that borrowing (excluding borrowings to finance a specific purpose or building)

The amount of borrowing costs capitalised could be **limited** because the **carrying amount of the asset including borrowing costs** should not exceed the asset's **recoverable amount**

Commencement of capitalisation

Capitalisation of borrowing costs should commence when the entity meets all 3 of the following conditions

- it incurs expenditure on the asset
- it incurs borrowing costs

Borrowing costs

it undertakes activities that are necessary to prepare the asset for its intended use

Activities include construction, drawing up plans, obtaining planning permissions, obtaining permissions from utility providers and obtaining other consents required – simply **holding** an asset for **development** without any associated activities is not enough to qualify for capitalisation

(Make sure you **illustrate** each condition with an **example** from the **exam scenario** at the same time that you define the above points – this is to ensure that you do not write things twice and waste time.)

Cessation of capitalisation

Capitalisation should cease when **substantially all** the activities necessary to get the asset ready for its intended use or sale are complete – minor activities such as decoration to a purchaser's specification do not form part of the substantial activities

Availability for sale is what matters, not the actual use or sale – availability for sale normally depends on the asset being physically complete

Building is constructed in parts – if each part is capable of being used/sold separately whilst other parts continue to be constructed, the cessation of capitalisation of borrowing costs should be assessed on the completion of each part – where no part is capable of being used/sold separately until all other parts have been completed, cessation should take place when the last part is completed

Deduction of investment income

Remember to deduct investment income received on invested funds from the total amount capitalised

Remember to state the amount that can be capitalised net of these funds i.e. actually do the calculation for the client

No depreciation

In the question, the asset is probably not yet complete so no depreciation should be charged as it is not ready for use

Disclosure

Costs which have been capitalised in the current period

Capitalisation rate used to determine the amount of borrowing costs eligible for capitalisation

Judgements required

Substantial period of time to get ready

Borrowing costs which are directly attributable

Activities necessary to prepare the qualifying asset

Substantially all the activities necessary are complete

Cash Flow Statement – Example

We provide an example Cash Flow Statement to provide you with basic reminders of issues to consider and where these should be recognised – other entries are of course possible

Ensure that you have practised the use of T-accounts to determine cash amounts paid or received

Remember to mention precisely **where** items should be disclosed in the Cash Flow Statement to create a well explained contrast with the P&L treatment which will apply an accruals approach (e.g. cash amounts in relation to pensions, finance leases, government grants etc)

Cash flows from operating activities

Cash generated from operations (reconciled in a note – see next page for an example)

Interest paid

Income taxes paid

Net cash from operating activities

Cash flows from investing activities

Purchase of property, plant and equipment

Proceeds from the sale of property, plant and equipment

Interest received

Dividends received

Net cash used in investing activities

Cash flows from financing activities

Proceeds from issue of share capital

Proceeds from issue of long-term borrowings

Dividends paid

Net cash used in financing activities

Net increase in cash and cash equivalents

Cash and cash equivalents at beginning of period

Cash and cash equivalents at end of period

Cash Flow Statement – Example

Example of a reconciliation note to find Cash generated from operations

This note provides some examples as reminders – other entries may be possible

Profit before tax	X
Depreciation charges	X
Loss on disposal of non-current assets	X
Interest expense	X
Increase in inventories	(X)
Decrease in receivables	X
Increase in payables	X
Cash generated from operations	**X**

Remember to add back non-cash expenses such as depreciation or a loss on disposal on non-current assets as these expenses do not require **cash** to be paid out

Add back interest expense because this amount is based on an accruals approach rather than the **cash** paid – you will deduct the **cash** paid in relation to interest in the next row of the SCF (see previous page)

For the working capital entries (inventories, receivables and payables) think about whether the movement is **good** or **bad** for the business

> **Inventories** – do we want to build up inventories or do we want to sell items rather than holding them? We want to sell rather than put money into inventories so an **increase** in inventories is **bad** and therefore a **negative** cash flow entry

> **Receivables** – we want receivables to **decline** as this means we are getting more cash in (rather than extending credit to customers via the receivables) so if receivables **increase** this is **bad** and therefore a **negative** cash flow entry

> **Payables** – we want to delay paying suppliers for as long as possible (without upsetting them) so a **decline** in payables would be **bad** and therefore a **negative** cash flow entry as it implies that we are settling bills more quickly

(In reality, we would also need to look at the relative amount of business we are doing to determine whether the movement really is good or bad but the above rules of thumb will always help to determine the correct movement (i.e. whether a positive or negative sign is needed.))

Consolidated Statement of Changes in Equity (CSoCIE)

As student performance on the CSoCIE (and single company SoCIE) tends to be poor (according to examiner comments), we include some notes here – you should also ensure that you can handle the more familiar CSFP and CSPL.

Example CSoCIE (figures are purely illustrative and may not reflect any relevant percentage holdings)

	Share capital	Retained earnings	Revaluation surplus	AFS Reserve	Total	NCI	Total
		Attributable to the owners of Example plc					
b/f at 1 Jan 2018	200,000	500,000	100,000	50,000	850,000	25,000	875,000
Total comprehensive income for the year		200,000		5,000	205,000	5,000	210,000
Added on acquisition in year						2,000	2,000
Dividends		(20,000)			(20,000)	(6,000)	(26,000)
c/f at 31 Dec 2018	200,000	680,000	100,000	55,000	1,035,000	26,000	1,061,000

Other reserves could include Shares to be issued (on acquisition of a subsidiary under an agreement to issue shares in future), share premium or a translation reserve, for example.

NCI

There will **nearly always** be entries for NCI's share of the subsidiary's total comprehensive income for the year and dividends paid/payable

There will **sometimes** be entries for the subsidiary's revaluations of non-current assets

If a partly-owned subsidiary is acquired during the year there will be an entry for NCI added on the acquisition of a subsidiary (and likewise eliminated on any disposal during the year)

NCI brought forward will be the NCI share of the subsidiary's equity brought forward or fair value plus NCI share of the subsidiary's post-acquisition reserves

Retained earnings brought forward

Group reserves brought forward = P's reserves brought forward + P% of subsidiary's post-acquisition reserves brought forward +/- goodwill impairment (to start of the year) and any other adjustments to the opening position

Customer loyalty programmes

Note – for ease of reference, we have simply copied across our notes on customer loyalty programmes from our **Revenue Recognition – IFRS 15** section of this book as there are no further points to be aware of, based on the available model answers reviewed for the purposes of creating the 2019 edition of this book

Suggested mark allocation in an FR question (CR Q2): 4 marks

Reward or loyalty points provide a material right to customers that they would not receive without entering into a contract

Therefore, the promise to provide goods and services to the customer in exchange for points is a performance obligation under IFRS 15

The total revenue received must be apportioned between the underlying sales and the related reward points, based on stand-alone prices

The allocation should also take into account the likelihood of customers actually claiming the points – for example, if there are total reward points with a face value of £5 million at the year-end but only 2 in 5 customers are expected to actually redeem their points then the value of the points should be calculated as £2 million (i.e. £5m x 2 / 5)

Once the correct value of the reward points (taking into account the probability of actual claim) has been calculated, this should be added to the revenue on the underlying sales for apportionment purposes – for example, if there is total underlying revenue of £100 million on equipment sales plus £2m of loyalty point value (after taking into account the probability of actual claim) then the allocation would be as follows:

Equipment sales	100 / 102 x 100	98.04
Loyalty points	2 / 102 x 100	1.96
		100.00

In substance, customers are implicitly paying for the reward points they receive when they buy other goods and services and hence some of the total revenue should be allocated to the points as a separate performance obligation

In the above example, £98.04 million would be recognised as revenue for the year and the balance of £1.96 million would be recognised as a contract liability (deferred revenue) in the SFP until the reward points are actually redeemed

Deferred tax

Suggested mark allocation in an FR question (CR Q2): 2 marks per issue (therefore work quickly and aim to at least cover all issues to some extent rather than concentrating on only certain areas)

Treatment

Choice of tax rate to apply

IAS 12 states that the tax rate to be used is the rate expected to apply when the asset is realised or the liability settled

This should be based upon laws already **enacted** or **substantively enacted** by the year end

Journals

To record an increase in a deferred tax asset

Debit   Deferred tax asset (SFP)

Credit Tax charge (P&L*)

To record an increase in a deferred tax liability

Debit   Tax charge (P&L*)

Credit Deferred tax liability (SFP)

Per the Corporate Reporting Study Manual, deferred tax assets and deferred tax liabilities should not be classified as current assets or liabilities even if the assets or liabilities are expected to be realised within 12 months

* Note that if the underlying transaction is recognised in equity through OCI, then the resulting deferred tax is included in OCI rather than the P&L as the deferred tax follows the underlying accounting treatment – for example, revalued assets under the IAS 16 revaluation model

Development costs

Check the question wording carefully to determine how these are treated in the foreign country

In many cases, the expenses are allowed for tax purposes at the time they are paid – however, for accounts purposes, if the costs are being capitalised then they will not be deducted for accounting profit purposes until the project commences and amortisation is charged

The **tax benefit** has therefore been taken **before** the **accounting benefit** and so a deferred tax **liability** arises, based on the carrying amount of the project valued at the applicable tax rate

Deferred tax

Fair value adjustments on a business combination

IFRS 3 requires recognition of net assets at FV but a revaluation upwards does not change the tax base of an asset – the revaluation is only recognised by tax authorities on disposal or generation of taxable income from the asset

A **revaluation upwards** therefore results in a **deferred tax liability** in the group financial statements – this will **increase** goodwill because there will be a bigger difference between consideration paid and the net assets acquired (since we have now found another liability to deduct from the net assets)

The liability will be equal to the difference between the revalued carrying amount and the unchanged tax base, multiplied by the relevant tax rate

Note that if the revaluation is recognised in OCI (e.g. revaluation of PPE) then the related deferred tax adjustment should also be recognised through OCI

Example – an asset with a carrying amount of 6 is revalued to its FV of 8 as part of a business combination

The carrying amount in the group financial statements will be 8 but the tax base will remain at 6 so there is a temporary difference of 2, to be valued at the tax rate applicable to the entity

No adjustment is required in the company's **individual** accounts as no FV adjustment is required – this matter only affects the **group accounts**

Recognition of goodwill on acquisition does not give rise to any deferred tax

Leases

In the case of a finance lease, the asset is written off over its useful life and a finance cost is recognised at a constant rate on the carrying amount of the liability

For tax purposes, relief is normally given as rentals are paid – the **tax base is nil** as there is no asset (TWDV value) for tax purposes and relief will be given in future as payments are made

Therefore there is likely to be a **deferred tax asset**, representing the tax recoverable in future – total rental payments which are deductible for tax purposes are likely to exceed the total depreciation of the asset because the rental payments must cover the costs of purchasing the asset and also cover the finance charge on top of the cost of the asset itself whereas depreciation is based only on the initial capitalised amount and does not include any element of finance charge

Tax losses – future expected profitability

It may be possible to recognise a **deferred tax asset** of an amount equal to tax losses incurred, valued at the applicable tax rate

However, there must be a **reasonable prospect of future profitability** – the deferred tax asset can only be recognised **to the extent that the losses are likely to be offset against future profits** (but subject to the January 2017 amendment discussed in the next sub-section)

Therefore, if it appears that the entity is unlikely to realise profits in the future due to poor underlying performance, no deferred tax asset should be recognised

Deferred tax

It may be necessary to recognise only **some** of the losses as a deferred tax asset i.e. only to the extent that they can be matched with likely future profits – this is quite a common point in the exam and could link into auditing/ethics if there is a suggestion that management are being too optimistic about future profitability in order to boost the company's asset base and/or in order to take a Credit to the P&L in relation to the deferred tax asset as a way of boosting accounting profit

Tax losses – company reporting a tax loss (January 2017 amendment)

Under an amendment effective from January 2017, a special calculation is performed to determine the deferred tax asset for a company reporting a tax loss – see the following example, which is based on the example on page 1285 and page 1286 of the 2019 edition of the Corporate Reporting Study Manual

A company has a deductible temporary difference of £400,000 and a taxable temporary difference of £120,000. The company expects the bottom line of its tax return to show a tax loss of £80,000.

Step 1 – determine whether there is a **taxable temporary difference** to support the recognition of a deferred tax asset – the company has a taxable temporary difference of **£120,000** so **at least** this amount can be recognised as a deferred tax asset

Step 2 – **special calculation** of taxable profit for recognition test

Expected tax loss per bottom line of tax return	(80)
less reversing taxable temporary difference	(120)
plus reversing deductible temporary difference	400
Taxable profit for recognition test	200

Step 3 – **add together** amounts from **Steps 1** and **2** – the company can therefore recognise a deferred tax asset of £120,000 + £200,000 = £320,000

This should be valued at the relevant tax rate.

This deferred tax asset would be recognised even though the company has an expected loss in its tax return.

Pensions – P&L and OCI split

In many tax jurisdictions, **pensions** are only **deductible** for **tax purposes** when **actually paid out** to recipients

A deferred tax **asset** will arise on the difference between the **net pension liability** and the **tax base of nil** (no tax deduction until actually paid in a future period)

In practice, most pension schemes record a net pension **liability** (i.e. a large amount to pay out in future, which will yield future tax deductibility) so there will be a deferred tax **asset** adjustment at the year end – the Credit side of this adjustment will go to the P&L

Remember that **actuarial gains and losses** must be recognised through **OCI** and deferred tax adjustments **follow** the accounting treatment so **deferred tax adjustments** on **actuarial gains and losses** must **also** be recognised through **OCI**

Deferred tax

In practice, most pension schemes record an actuarial **loss** for the year, so there will be a deferred tax **asset** adjustment which goes through **OCI**

You may therefore have to carefully split an overall deferred tax asset adjustment into its P&L and OCI **components** (credit the P&L in relation to the net pension liability element **and** OCI in relation to the actuarial loss element)– see Corporate Reporting Question Bank Q2 **Mervyn** for an example of this process

PPE

The **accounting carrying amount** of PPE is the **net book value** of the assets – this is reduced gradually based on **depreciation**

The **tax base** is the tax written down value – this is reduced gradually based on the **capital allowance** rate

It is unlikely that the depreciation rate will be the same as the capital allowance rate – this gives rise to a temporary difference

If the **tax base exceeds the carrying amount**, there will be a **deferred tax asset** as over the remaining life of the asset there will be more tax deductions received (which would reduce taxable profits) than depreciation to add back (which would increase taxable profits) – overall, the entity will see a **net deduction** from the tax charge

If the **tax base is lower than the carrying amount**, there will be a **deferred tax liability** as over the remaining life of the asset there will be fewer tax deductions (which would reduce taxable profits) than depreciation to add back (which would increase taxable profits) – overall, the entity will see a **net addition** to the tax charge. Put another way, too much tax relief has already been granted relative to the accounts carrying amount and this needs to be reversed

Calculate the difference between the carrying amount and tax base at the year end and create a deferred tax asset or liability as required, per the above. Then check to see what the opening liability or asset was – only the necessary **change** is charged this year.

PPE – Revaluation

This creates a **deferred tax liability** – there is no increase in the tax base from a revaluation but the carrying amount in the accounts will increase

The charge to increase the deferred tax liability should be recognised in **OCI** and not in **profit or loss**

Interaction with IAS 40

If the property is held under the FV model, gains are recognised through **profit or loss** and taxable at the same time (or in the case of a loss, allowable for tax at the same time) so there is **no deferred tax** to consider as there is **no timing mismatch** – however, if the item is held under the cost model or the revaluation model under IAS 16 then revaluation gains are recognised through OCI and therefore are not taxed at the time, giving rise to a deferred tax liability – remember that this deferred tax should follow the underlying item and be recognised in OCI and not in the current tax account in the P&L

Deferred tax

Provisions

Often provisions will relate to future accounting periods (remember to apply discounting if this would make a material difference) – an expense will be **recognised** for accounting purposes but the amounts will not be deductible for **tax purposes** until they are actually paid in **future**

The entity will therefore receive a **future tax benefit** so a **deferred tax asset** is created, based on the estimated present value of the provision valued at the applicable tax rate

Share-based payment

Normally, **tax** authorities do not give relief for share-based payments **until exercise** – this contrasts with the accounts treatment where there will be an **annual expense** posted with an equivalent increase in equity to be issued (or liabilities for a cash-settled scheme) each year

This will create a **deferred tax asset** because the entity will have a future tax deduction which has not yet been claimed

The accounts carrying amount of the share-based payment expense will be nil because the expense is recognised in full each year

The tax base of the share-based payments will be based on

> options x employees x proportion of employees expected to qualify x intrinsic value x fraction for the relevant year (e.g. 1/3 in the first year of a 3 year vesting period, 2/3 in the second year and so on)
>
> Intrinsic value is the difference between the market price and the exercise price under the option

Therefore the temporary difference will be **equal to the tax base** as the carrying amount for accounts purposes is **nil**

Deferred tax that relates to the **excess** of intrinsic value over fair value at the grant date should be recognised in **equity** – therefore if the tax deduction **exceeds** the accounting deduction put the excess through **equity** and not the P&L

Unrealised profit (PURPs)

The tax authorities tax a sale regardless of whether it is internal or external to the group – taxation is based on individual company profit figures, not the group figures

In the group accounts, unrealised profits on goods sold internally which remain in inventories must be cancelled – this means that the accounts carrying amount of inventory in the group accounts will be lower than the tax base of those inventories, because of the deduction of the PURP

Therefore there will be a **deferred tax asset** equal to the difference between the carrying amount in the group accounts and the tax base, valued at the tax rate applicable to the entity – the reason is that the tax authorities will **already have charged tax** on the sale of those inventories by the individual company because the fact that the sales were intra-group is not relevant for tax purposes: the group can therefore earn future profits without incurring tax so a **deferred tax asset arises** – therefore it is necessary to reduce the group's tax charge to match the accounting treatment where profit was reduced when adjusting for the PURP

This is because tax has been charged on profit which is non-existent from the group perspective

Deferred tax

Unremitted earnings

Unremitted earnings potentially create a deferred tax liability – the group accounts consolidate the profit of subsidiaries but this is not recognised for tax purposes: rather, additional tax could be due when the earnings are remitted from the subsidiary to the parent

However, IAS 12 states that no deferred tax liability should be recognised if the parent company controls the timing of the subsidiary's dividend distribution and it is probable that the temporary difference will not reverse in the foreseeable future as the parent intends to leave the profits within the subsidiary for reinvestment purposes

DEPS

Suggested mark allocation in an FR question (CR Q2): 4-5 marks

Provides useful information to users by relating **current** earnings to the possible **future** capital structure (i.e. future number of shares that could exist)

DEPS allows for both the impact on earnings of the issued shares and also the impact of an increased number of shares

Could be used as part of a PE valuation to show the impact on future valuation if instruments are converted into equity

Limitations

Uses **current** earnings but **future** number of shares – the current earnings figure may not be relevant in future years – the level of earnings at the time of conversion is what matters

Assumes that all potential diluting financial instruments will be converted into shares – this may not happen as some debt holders may redeem the instrument for cash, rather than converting into shares, or share options may lapse if holders leave the company

DEPS can therefore only be an **indicator** regarding potential future events – it is not a **forecast** of future earnings

Antidilution

If potential ordinary shares would **increase** EPS (or decrease the loss per share) then they are **antidilutive** and are not taken into account for DEPS purposes

Each issue or series of potential ordinary shares is considered **separately** rather than in aggregate

> Ignore any shares that increase EPS or decrease the loss per share as these are automatically antidilutive

> Rank dilutive instruments from most to least dilutive – options and warrants are generally included first because they do not affect the numerator (top half or profit element) of the EPS calculation – dilutive factors are added one by one into the DEPS calculation in order to identify the maximum dilution

Calculation of diluted earnings

Take profit or loss attributable to **ordinary** equity holders and adjust this for the **after-tax** effect of

> Any dividends or other items relating to dilutive potential ordinary shares deducted in arriving at profit or loss attributable to ordinary equity holders

> Any interest recognised in the period relating to dilutive potential ordinary shares

DEPS

Any other changes in income or expense that would result from the conversion of the dilutive potential ordinary shares

Calculation of number of shares

Treat dilution as occurring at the **start of the period** or, if later as a result of an issue during the current year, the date of issue of the potential ordinary shares

If there is more than one basis of conversion then assume the most advantageous rate of conversion from the standpoint of the holder

Convertible instruments

Increase earnings by interest saved, net of tax

Increase number of shares by the number of shares created by the conversion

Options and warrants (other than employee share options)

Apply a split calculation – shares issued at average market price are ignored but **free shares** are added into the calculation

Calculation of "free shares" – example

Exercise price is £0.50, average market price is £1.50 and number of shares under option is 600,000

Free element is £1.00 / £1.50 x 600,000 or 400,000

Ignore the other 200,000 shares for DEPS purposes

Employee share options

In the case of vested shares, apply a "free share" approach as above (see Options and warrants above)

In the case of unvested shares, apply the same general method but first find the per share amount still to be recognised in the P&L relating to the share options and add this to the exercise price in the calculation before proceeding as normal using a free shares calculation

Example

Exercise price is £21 in relation to 5m shares with £15m to be recognised – average market price is £30

The per share amount still to be recognised is £15m / 5m = £3 so exercise price now treated as £21 + £3 or £24

"Free shares" therefore based on £30 - £24 = 6 / 30 x shares under option

Contingently issuable shares

Do not include in EPS unless actually issued

Include for DEPS if and only if the conditions leading to their issue are satisfied, treating the end of the current accounting period as if it were the end of the contingency period (i.e. look at whether the conditions would be satisfied assuming that nothing were to change between the current accounting period and ultimate end date)

> If necessary to include, include from the beginning of the period, or, if later, from the date of the contingent share agreement if this was entered into during the year

Examples of performance criteria: future earnings, market price of shares, future earnings & market price of shares

If the performance criteria involve a **cumulative target** then no dilution is accounted for until the cumulative target has been met – for example, for a target of **average profits of £100,000 over 5 years** then the cumulative target required is £500,000 so no DEPS impact occurs until the cumulative target is met i.e. towards the end of the process rather than each year

As always with DEPS, assume that the shares were issued at the **start** of the year (only assume a later date if the agreement was entered into during the current accounting period)

Equity-settled share scheme

Normally it is necessary to take account of the number of "free" shares being allocated, assuming that the whole scheme will vest

Where options are not yet vested, there should also be an adjustment to the option exercise price based on the remaining IFRS 2 cost to be expensed in future – calculate what this is on a per share basis and add it to the exercise price before calculating the number of "free shares" in the normal way (see previous page)

If there is a **performance condition** (other than the mere passage of time) such as a share price condition then treat the shares as contingently issuable shares

> IAS 33 states that "the calculation of diluted EPS is based on the number of ordinary shares that would be issued if the market price at the end of the reporting period were the market price at the end of the contingency period" – therefore it is possible that there may not be dilution if the condition is not met at the year end

See also our section on **EPS** starting on **page 48**.

Derivatives and Embedded Derivatives

Suggested mark allocation in an FR question (CR Q2): 4 marks

Derivative – Definition

Value changes in response to the change in price of an underlying security, commodity, currency, index or other financial instrument(s)

Initial net investment is zero or is small in relation to the value of the underlying security or index

Settled at a future date

Tips

Make sure you always review the above 3 criteria for a derivative to exist – make sure you connect these to the scenario through **examples**

Accounting treatment

Recognise a derivative initially at fair value – do not forget to add on the **initial cost**, if any (see below), but do not add any **transaction fees**

Dr Financial asset

Cr Cash/Payables

Treat any **transaction** costs as an expense in the P&L – however, the **cost of the instrument** itself (e.g. a **premium** on an option) should be **capitalised** into the cost of the asset on the SFP i.e. it should **not** be expensed – therefore just expense **transaction costs** such as professional fees

Update the instrument for fair value at the SFP date – the change in fair value should be recognised in profit or loss

Example of the journals for a **gain** on a derivative in the year

Dr Financial asset

Cr Operating income (P&L)

Example of the journals for a **loss** on a derivative in the year

Dr Operating income (P&L)

Cr Financial asset

Embedded Derivatives – Definition

A derivative component of a hybrid (combined) instrument that also includes a non-derivative host contract

Exam tip – if the exam paper provides you with a **separately** stated FV of an instrument if it were purchased on its own then this is a strong indicator that an **embedded** derivative exists as you are being given a figure to **split out**

Example host contracts

Leases, debt or equity instruments, insurance contracts, sale or purchase contracts, construction contracts

The contract must involve terms such that the embedded derivative cannot be detached and sold to a third party – if it can be, it is simply a separate financial instrument

An investment in a debt instrument that is convertible into ordinary shares of the issuer – the debt instrument is the host contract and the conversion option is the embedded derivative

A debt instrument with an extension option with the interest rate in the extension period reset to 1.2 times the market rate – the debt instrument is the host contract with the extension option involving an embedded derivative

A lease contract which has a rent adjustment clause based on changes in the local inflation rate – the lease is the host contract with inflation-related rentals being the embedded derivative

Treatment

Determine (1) if the **economic** characteristics and risks of the embedded derivative are **not closely related** to the economic characteristics and risks of the host contract (2) whether a **separate** instrument with the **same terms** as the embedded derivative would meet the definition of a derivative and (3) whether the **hybrid contract** is not already being accounted for at FVtPL

Separate out the derivative from its host contract and treat as a normal derivative – this ensures that the entity cannot **hide** the derivative outside of the P&L

The entity may **choose** to **designate** a hybrid contract at FVtPL, avoiding the need to **split out** the embedded derivative

Examples of embedded derivatives/not closely related instruments

A bond which is redeemable in 5 years' time with part of the redemption price being based on the increase in the FTSE 100 Index

A construction contract priced in a foreign currency – the construction contract is a non-derivative contract but the changes in the foreign exchange rate involve an embedded derivative

Cash flows of the host contract are modified by an index, specified interest rate, foreign exchange rate, index of price or rates etc – i.e. something which has no real connection with the contract

Derivatives and Embedded Derivatives

Convertible bond – a mixture of a normal bond (host contract) and a call option (embedded derivative) that gives the holder of the bond the right to exchange the bond for shares in the company

Currency involved is different from the functional currency of both parties (unless the items in the transaction are routinely denominated in the currency involved in international commerce)

Option to extend the term on a fixed debt instrument without resetting the interest rate to market rates

Credit derivatives in a debt instrument

Put option enabling the holder to require the issuer to reacquire the instrument for a value that varies on the basis of a change in an equity or commodity price or index

From the point of view of the holder only, a call option embedded in an equity instrument that enables the issuer to reacquire that equity instrument at a specified price

Equity-indexed interest or principal payments embedded in a host debt instrument or insurance contract

An equity conversion feature embedded in a convertible debt instrument

A call, put or prepayment option embedded in a host debt contract or host insurance contract

Distributable Profits

The basic rule

Distributable profits are accumulated realised profits less accumulated realised losses

For **listed** companies, distributable profits are **further** reduced by the excess of unrealised losses over unrealised profits

> Listed companies must also not make a distribution if this reduces net assets below the total of called-up share capital and undistributable reserves

> Undistributable reserves are the share premium account, net unrealised profits and other reserves specified by law or the company's constitution to be unrealised e.g. a capital redemption reserve

Realised or unrealised?

Companies Act 2006 provides specific guidance.

> A provision is a realised loss

> A revaluation surplus is an unrealised profit

> Additional depreciation on revalued non-current assets can be added back to profits for the purposes of determining distributable amounts

> Where a revalued asset is disposed of, the unrealised surplus or loss on revaluation becomes a realised profit or loss

> Revaluation gains are unrealised unless they reverse a loss previously treated as realised

> Losses are realised except where the loss offsets a previous surplus on the same asset or arises on a revaluation of all non-current assets or arises on a revaluation of some non-current assets where the directors consider that the assets not revalued are worth at least their book value

ICAEW/ICAS Technical Release 02/10

The translation of monetary assets which comprise qualifying consideration or a liability denominated in a foreign currency is a realised profit

Goodwill arising in a company's individual financial statements will become a realised loss as the goodwill is amortised or written down for impairment in accordance with the relevant accounting standards

Negative goodwill (gain on a bargain purchase) up to the FV of the non-monetary assets acquired should be treated as being realised in the periods in which the non-monetary assets are recovered, whether through depreciation or sale

Group calculation?

The calculation must be done for each entity separately and not for the consolidated group – the consolidated group only exists for accounting purposes

Note that the legality of a dividend distribution is determined by the distributable profits in the **separate** financial statements of a single company rather than by **consolidated** retained earnings

It is possible for group retained earnings to be negative due to losses in subsidiaries but with an individual parent company having a positive retained earnings balance due to its own profitability – this would allow payment of a dividend to the parent company's shareholders

EPS

Suggested mark allocation in an FR question (CR Q2): 2 marks

Compliance with IAS 33 on EPS is mandatory for the **separate** financial statements of entities whose ordinary shares are **publicly traded** or are in the **process of being issued** in public markets and for the **consolidated** financial statements for groups whose parent has shares similarly traded/being issued

Other entities need not present EPS – if their shares are not traded there is no readily available market price to calculate the PE ratio (the reason why EPS figures are quoted)

Presentation

EPS should be presented in the P&L (DEPS should also be presented with equal prominence, if needed)

Basic calculation

Profit or loss attributable to ordinary equity holders of the parent / weighted average number of ordinary shares outstanding during the period

To calculate the profit or loss figure used here, remember to treat **redeemable** preference shares as liabilities and as such these involve a **finance charge** that should **already have been deducted** in the P&L (so no adjustment needed if the client has used the right approach) – but remember to then deduct the amount of any **dividend on irredeemable** preference shares (as EPS works on the basis of profit or loss attributable to **ordinary** shares)

In the case of cumulative dividends on irredeemable preference shares then

If the dividend is not paid in the year, deduct it from profit for the EPS calculation

When the arrears of past dividends are paid, exclude from the EPS calculation

Rights issue

See separate **Rights issue** topic on **page 173**.

Bonus fraction

The terms work on the basis for "new for old" – a 2 for 1 bonus issue means that 2 new shares are issued for every 1 existing or old share already held – the bonus fraction would then be 3 / 1 (holder now has 3 shares and had 1 before)

Remember that this means you should always have a **higher** number on the top of the fraction than on the **bottom** of the fraction

Remember to treat bonus issues as if the relevant shares have always existed i.e. go right back in time over the full current year and also as against the prior year

EPS

Remember that a quick way to find the **prior year** comparative EPS after a bonus issue is to apply the **reciprocal** of this year's bonus fraction to last year's **EPS** – this will have the effect of pushing down last year's EPS as we are now assuming that more shares always existed (with earnings last year unchanged, EPS must now be lower when allowing for the new bonus shares as the same amount of earnings is being spread over a greater number of shares)

Careful – if you are told last year's **earnings** (rather than **EPS**) then you cannot use this reciprocal approach – instead you will need to calculate the total number of shares and divide last year's earnings by that number of shares – therefore always check carefully whether you have been told EPS or rather total earnings

Issue at full market price

Only consider this on a **prospective** basis – do **not** go backwards and update the number of shares

There is no need for any complicated fraction as with a bonus or rights issue – simply add in the number of shares from the relevant date and pro-rate this (as the issue will almost certainly happen during the year)

Profit attributable to ordinary equity holders

Profit after tax after the deduction of preference dividends and other financing costs

Partly paid shares

Treat these as a fraction of a share, based on their ability to participate in dividends

So if 600 shares are issued at a £4 price but only £2 has been paid than apply a fraction of 2 / 4 to the share issue, treating it as an issue of 300 shares (not 600)

See also our section on **DEPS** starting on **page 40**

Ethics

Suggested mark allocation in an FR question (CR Q2): 8 marks

The 5 threats

Intimidation threat

Self-interest threat

Self-review threat

Management threat

Advocacy threat

The 5 ICAEW Code Principles

Integrity – being straightforward and honest in all professional and business relationships

Objectivity – not allowing bias, conflicts of interest or undue influence of others to override a professional judgement

Professional competence and due care – only perform work that one is competent to perform

Confidentiality – not to disclose information to third parties without proper and specific authority

Professional behaviour – compliance with laws and regulations and avoidance of any action that discredits the profession

Example Ethics scenarios from Corporate Reporting past papers

1. Acting as auditor during a possible takeover or within a group – confidentiality

2. Acting on overheard information

3. AIM-listed company

4. Audit firm to provide additional assurance services

5. Audit manager leaves the firm to work as a director at an audit client

6. Application of pressure to the auditor – materiality, fees, timing

7. Corruption allegations by an ex-employee of an audit client in a newspaper article

8. Cyber attack with less than full transparency from the client

9. Dominance of a Board member

10. Fee income levels

11. Identification of errors in corporation tax return

12. Late appointment as auditor

Ethics

13. No Finance Director in place

14. Personal relationships between audit team members and client staff

15. Possible fraud

16. Quality of work performed

17. Requesting the audit firm to assist in calculating entries

18. Taxation issues – transfer pricing

1. Acting as auditor during a possible takeover or within a group – confidentiality

As auditors of an entity, we may have access to confidential information which would be of use to another party in assessing the value or probability of various matters e.g. the probability of contingent consideration being payable or the fair value of assets and liabilities

This creates a conflict of interest – we must ensure that confidential information cannot be passed from one company to the other

Within a group situation, the potential conflict of interest should be disclosed to the relevant audit committee

It may be necessary to arrange independent partner reviews of the group and individual entity audit files

2. Acting on overheard information

Overheard information contains no actual evidence and could be no more than malicious gossip without foundation in fact

Even so, the accountant who has heard the information is not entitled to ignore it completely – the accountant should investigate the allegations as discreetly as possible – there may be a criminal dimension

If the issue could be defined as money laundering then the accountant must take care that enquiries do not "tip off" any relevant individuals

Once the relevant facts have been gathered, it may be appropriate to escalate the matter – it may be worth contacting ICAEW for help in determining whether or not the matter should be taken forward, what kind of evidence is required and what action would be most appropriate

All ICAEW Chartered Accountants are bound by the ICAEW Ethical Code and must act with integrity in all circumstances and must display professional behaviour – otherwise this could bring the profession into disrepute

There may be internal procedures to deal with the allegations at the client company – if the company is listed it should have appointed Non-Executive Directors but if it is unlisted it may still have this kind of Director anyway

It may be appropriate to approach the chair of the audit committee, provided that the accountant is very certain of the facts and the allegations are presented carefully

At all stages a detailed record of investigations, deliberations and conclusions may be required as evidence in the event of criminal and/or professional disciplinary action

Ethics

3. AIM-listed company

Not required to make disclosures of compliance with the provisions of the UK Corporate Governance Code

ISA 260 requires matters of concern to be raised with those charged with governance – audit committee would be the point of contact

Information in the published financial statements should be reviewed for consistency with appropriate professional scepticism being applied

4. Audit firm to provide additional assurance services

Such an assignment would be called a "non-audit related service"

The firm should identify any threats to independence and objectivity

> A low fee for the work could be a threat to independence

The relative size of the engagement fee in relation to the audit fee should be considered and discussed with the ethics partner

There may also be a risk that the firm would end up auditing its own work

Consider if the firm is being pressurised by the client in any way

The firm should not undertake work in which it does not have the expertise – ICAEW Chartered Accountants must act in accordance with professional competence and behaviour

The firm must consider the nature of the non-audit services involved – further information may be required on timing, nature and extent of the work, likely level of fees and the fee basis

Must guard against "low-balling" on audit work in order to win non-audit work

5. Audit manager leaves the firm to work as a director at an audit client

If the audit manager is a Chartered Accountant then he or she is required to follow the principles and spirit of the ICAEW Code and to act at all times with integrity, objectivity and professional competence and due care

If a cold review is critical of an audit in which the audit manager was involved before his or her departure from the firm to join the client who was the focus of that audit, this could raise potential questions about the diligence and focus on detail of the audit manager (whilst recognising that ultimate responsibility for the audit documentation has to lie with the audit partner) – it is possible that the audit manager was contemplating or even discussing his or her move to the client while working on the audit, causing his or her judgement to have been influenced by the desire to please a future potential employer

Questions should have arisen at the firm at the point when the audit manager announced his or her resignation and there may have been conversations with the partner at the time that the audit manager started to pursue the opportunity at the client – more information may therefore be available and required in order to assess whether the audit manager acted with an appropriate level of integrity and openness

The firm may wish to consider the scope of the cold review and the need to look again at any areas of the file which were not reviewed, particularly in relation to the audit manager who has left the firm

Incorrect adjustments could suggest either incompetence and lack of care or, alternatively, deliberate manipulation of the results – however, incorrect entries which understate profit may be less likely to be a result of deliberate manipulation as it would seem unlikely that the audit manager would have any incentive to deliberately include such errors

Actions: the engagement team will want to consult with the firm's ethics partner and possibly other senior partners within the firm – as the audit manager was not the audit partner on the audit, the firm can continue to act as auditor: however, as the audit manager was a member of the client engagement team and has joined the client as a key member of the executive team within 2 years of being involved with the audit, the firm should look at the composition of the audit team and ensure that it is appropriately independent of the departing audit manager and not made up of individuals who are close to him or her or accustomed to working under his or her instruction – it may therefore be necessary to change the composition of the audit team

If, having undertaken full enquiries to establish the facts, there is evidence that the audit manager has acted unethically or even fraudulently then the audit firm will need to report any breaches of the ICAEW code and consider the need to talk to the other directors of the client company

6. Application of pressure to the auditor – materiality, fees, timing

Auditors must act in the public interest as they have responsibilities to the users of the financial statements

Objectivity is threatened if there is pressure to increase materiality and reduce the amount of work required – professional judgement is threatened – auditor must determine materiality in an objective way, considering the needs of the users of the financial statements

Self-interest threat as auditor will want to retain work in future years but the client is requesting a reduction in audit time and costs to retain margin – must ensure that the auditor is not influenced by the wish to retain future work

Intimidation threat as client is suggesting that auditor may not be given other non-audit work in future – this could prevent objectivity and safeguards will need to be applied – risk of "low-balling" on audit work in order to win non-audit work

Actions: discuss with ethics partner at an early stage and arrange for an additional partner file review – advice from ICAEW ethics helpline – full documentation of any decisions on level of work and contentious issues – consider making changes to ensure an appropriate level and resilience of the audit team

7. Corruption allegations by an ex-employee of an audit client in a newspaper article

The evidence presented in a newspaper article must be questioned – it is important that the full facts are established

If claims have been made by a former employee, the audit firm may not have full or any knowledge of the circumstances nor of the credibility of the individual and the situation involved in their departure from the company – the allegations could be motivated by some form of ill-feeling towards a former employee

The claims made in the article may be well founded and the auditor should consider whether the review of the financial statements lends any credence to the allegations – further audit procedures should be performed

Ethics

Actions for the audit firm: consider the firm's reporting obligations under relevant tax and legal rules, including money laundering regulations – consider taking legal advice – consider whether bribery legislation could be relevant – discuss the matter with those charged with governance at the client to establish the facts – contact the firm's ethics partner and involve him or her in resolution of the issue – contact the ICAEW helpline – take care not to engage in any activity that could be construed as "tipping off" – consider whether the integrity of management is now questionable and whether the auditor therefore cannot place as much reliance on evidence from the management as was previously believed to be the case – consider whether there remains sufficient appropriate evidence to ground the audit opinion on the financial statements

Actions for a director who has already raised concerns regarding the allegations: as a director, the individual must not allow himself or herself to be associated with fraud or illegal activities (particularly if the individual is an ICAEW member) – the individual should discuss the matter with his or her board colleagues – the individual should be advised to consider his or her position at the company and whether he or she wants to continue to work for his or her current employer – if an ICAEW member, the individual should contact ICAEW for advice on how he or she should proceed

8. Cyber attack with less than full transparency from the client

Background: possible security breach so client accounts may have been accessed, but no evidence so far and therefore clients not informed – some clients might suffer a financial loss – disclosed in management commentary in the interim financial statements but not made public in any other way

Answer: appears to be a deliberate attempt to hold back information from the company's clients – could be a breach of requirements regarding the protection of client data

Lack of transparency, professional competence and due care – attempt by the Finance Director (ICAEW Chartered Accountant) to cover up could indicate weak corporate governance

Taken with other matters (management commentary states that gross profit margin has increased from 60% but does not say what figure it has increased to, prepayment of costs and bringing forward income), could suggest that the Finance Director is attempting to manipulate the accounts

Self-interest threat for assurance provider as will not want to jeopardise relationship with client

Actions: engagement partner should discuss with client's directors to establish the facts – consult ethics partner to consider whether there is a case for reporting a fellow ICAEW member (the Finance Director at the client) for a breach of the ICAEW Code – assurance provider should seek legal advice and could suffer reputational damage

9. Dominance of a Board member

Creates a governance issue but not necessarily an ethical issue

Needs to be separation between Chairperson and CEO

10. Fee income levels

Revised Ethical Standard 2016 upper bound of 15% of the firm's total fee income from an unlisted client

For a listed or Public Interest Entity (PIE) client, the limit falls to 10%

Ethics

If fees range from 5% to 10% for listed/PIE clients or 10% to 15% for non-listed clients, the fact needs to be disclosed to the ethics partner and those charged with governance at the client – appropriate safeguards should be adopted, including declining some of the work

11. Identification of errors in corporation tax return

Must follow the fundamental principles of the ICAEW Code – must not be associated with a tax return which the accountant knows to contain an error

Should report this to HMRC

Where a matter is in the public interest, duty to report to ICAEW any facts or matters indicating that a member or trainee member may have become liable to disciplinary action – deliberate underpayment of tax cannot be in the public interest so there may well be a duty to report

Disciplinary action could take place if the accountant does not act within the spirit of the Code

Ask the client to disclose the error to the tax authorities – if there is a refusal, the matter should be raised with those charged with governance at the client

Consider whether to continue to act for a client which has knowingly filed a false tax return

Consult the ethics partner throughout the deliberations

Could be reporting implications under the Money Laundering regulations because tax evasion results in criminal property – MLCP (Money Laundering Compliance Principal) should be consulted on whether disclosure to the NCA is needed – ensure no tipping off

Ensure that an appropriately experienced and skilled individual performs the audit work on tax balances as these are not straightforward

If the client refuses to make any adjustment, this potentially raises an intimidation threat – discuss with the assignment partner and the firm's ethics partner – raise the matter with those charged with governance and the relevant adjustments should be made to the financial statements

Other key threats: self-interest (fees from client), self-review (auditing tax computations it had prepared), management (auditor might become involved in tax planning – tax is a very technical area so can management be properly informed?)

Consider whether the audit firm wants to be associated with such a client, taking into account other errors – consider resignation

12. Late appointment as auditor

Check if this has occurred because of the resignation of a previous auditor – if this is the case, perhaps an issue was identified by that auditor and we should determine if this matter still applies – this should be discussed with the client

Ensure that adequate professional clearance has been obtained from the previous auditor and that there are no matters of which we should be aware

Ensure that satisfactory client identification procedures have been performed

Ethics

Check if we have been appointed as auditor after the year end – if this is the case, it may be more difficult to assess matters as they stood at the year-end – if we cannot implement audit procedures to gain sufficient audit evidence of the position at the year-end then the audit opinion will have to be modified

> If the possible errors are considered to be material, this may result in a qualified or "except for" opinion

> If the potential effect is pervasive, we may have to issue a "disclaimer" of opinion

13. No Finance Director in place

Need to ensure a Finance Director is in place rather than having CEO making all decisions

This could lead to ethical concerns such as pressure to produce good results or there may be a lack of good quality information and controls – there may also be an opportunity for people to make the most of the fact that an individual with significant supervisory responsibilities over controls is not in place

Greater likelihood of a management threat for the audit firm if it acts in the role of a Finance Director

14. Personal relationships between audit team members and client staff

If an individual is considered to be a close family member, then the member of the audit team may have to be removed from the team, particularly if the family member has a role such as a financial controller or director at the client – this is because the family member could exercise influence over the information submitted for audit

It would not matter if the close family member used to work for the audit firm unless he or she was a partner of the firm, in which case the audit appointment should not be accepted

15. Possible fraud

The auditor needs to determine whether there is collusion between staff and/or other entities (if applicable)

There is an ethical issue for the auditor if the client has unaddressed ethical issues as this increases engagement risk

The auditor should adopt an attitude of professional scepticism – the auditor should obtain relevant audit evidence of the impact of fraud-related issues and this should be documented including tests performed, discussions with audit team members and detailed enquiries made at the appropriate level of management together with their responses

If fraud is suspected, the entity should report to those responsible for governance at the appropriate level – note that key finance staff such as finance directors or finance controllers could be involved in the fraud so their actions should be given careful consideration

There may also be responsibilities under the money laundering legislation so there should be consultation with the firm's MLCP (Money Laundering Compliance Principal)

Ethics

16. Quality of work performed

The adviser must act in accordance with the ICAEW Code of Ethics in respect of professional competence and due care

Inadequate supervision of a junior member of staff would compromise the quality of work, especially if not identified on a timely basis – if there are problems on other assignments involving the same individual, this would be a further concern

Any evidence of poor or inadequate training would also suggest a lack of professional competence

17. Requesting the audit firm to assist in calculating entries

This would require the audit firm to ensure any threat of self-review can be mitigated

This can be achieved by using people from outside the audit team to assist or suggesting that parent company staff rather than audit firm staff provide assistance

The audit firm should also ensure that the financial controller and directors take full managerial responsibility for all assumptions made – in particular this includes judgemental assumptions which must definitely not be suggested by the audit firm or the firm will be playing a management role

Further ethical problems will arise if client staff lack expertise in a complex area – the auditor should be even more alert to the risks of misstatement and the fact that the audit firm may be asked to step in as this would lead to a management threat

18. Taxation issues – transfer pricing

Special deals with unusual rental fees may have been entered into to evade UK tax

Details and expert input from tax consultants in the overseas country needed

Report to the audit firm's Money Laundering Compliance Principal may be required

Events After the Reporting Period

Suggested mark allocation in an FR question (CR Q2): 5 marks

Treatment of an adjusting event

The event provides evidence of **conditions** that **existed** at the **end of the reporting period** – IAS 10 therefore applies

An accrual may be needed if we now have good evidence of the costs involved

Note that this could mean that a contingent liability in the draft accounts is now replaced and its related note removed as we have better evidence of the position as it stood at the end of the reporting period

There is no specific requirement to disclose the mere fact that the event is an adjusting event

Adjusting events after the reporting period (evidence of conditions at the reporting date)

Settlement of a court case that confirms that the entity had an obligation at the reporting date

Evidence that an asset was impaired at the reporting date e.g. bankruptcy of a customer or selling prices for inventory now sold

Determination of bonus payments or a profit-sharing agreement for the year

Finalisation of prices for assets sold/purchased before the year end

Discovery of material fraud or errors that show the financial statements are misstated

Adjustment to EPS for bonus issues, share splits or share consolidations where the number of shares changed without an increase in resources – the additional shares issued are treated as having been in issue for the whole period

Non-adjusting events after the reporting period (evidence of conditions that arose after the reporting date)

Such events should be disclosed where this would influence the economic decisions made by users of the financial statements but there is no need to recognise the amounts

A major business combination after the reporting date

Announcement of plan to discontinue an operation after the reporting date

Major purchases and disposals of assets after the reporting date

Classification of assets as held for sale after the reporting date

Expropriation of assets by government after the reporting date

Destruction of assets after the reporting date

Announcing or commencing the implementation of a major restructuring after the reporting date

Events After the Reporting Period

Major ordinary share transactions (unless no inflow or outflow of economic resources is involved) after the reporting date

Decline in the market value of investments including investment properties after the reporting date – these should not be affected by hindsight

Examples from past papers

Court case

If the court case was in progress at the year-end but has now been concluded and a specific monetary amount is known then an **adjusting** event occurs – we have good evidence of the cost of a matter in progress at the year end

Proposed dividend

Dividends are only recognised if they are declared before the end of the reporting period

The directors do not have any obligation to declare or pay a dividend at any time and therefore there cannot be a liability unless an announcement has been made

It is possible that a past record in relation to dividends could create a constructive obligation under IAS 37 but there would still need to be some action such as a proposal of a dividend by the end of the reporting period – otherwise, it is not recognised

If the proposed dividend was approved before the financial statements were authorised to issue, it should still be disclosed in the notes to the financial statements even though it is not recognised

Fair Value – IFRS 13

Suggested mark allocation in an FR question (CR Q2): 6 marks (relatively new topic and complex)

Definition under IFRS 13

The price that would be received to sell an asset or paid to transfer a liability in an orderly transaction between market participants at the measurement date

IFRS 13 does not apply (either in relation to **measurement** nor to **disclosures**) to

    Share-based payment transactions within the scope of IFRS 2

    Leasing transactions within the scope of IAS 17

    Net realisable value under IAS 2

IFRS 13 **disclosure** requirements do not apply to

    Plan assets measured at FV in accordance with IAS 19

    Plan investments measured at FV in accordance with IAS 26

    Assets for which the recoverable amount is FV less disposal costs under IAS 36

Measurement

It is assumed that the transaction would take place in the principal market or in the most advantageous market, in an orderly transaction rather than under a forced sale

FV is not adjusted for transaction costs but these can be taken into account when determining the most advantageous market

Non-financial assets are valued based on the use to which the asset can be put in its highest and best use

The use of bid prices for financial assets and the use of ask prices for financial liabilities is permitted, but not required – IFRS 13 does not preclude the use of mid-market pricing

Example measurement methods for liabilities and own equity instruments

Quoted price exists for an **identical or similar** liability/own equity instrument – use the **quoted** price

No quoted price exists for the transfer of an **identical or similar** liability/own equity instrument but there is an **identical item held by another entity as an asset** – measure the fair value of the liability or equity instrument from the **perspective of a market participant that holds the identical item as an asset** at the measurement date

No quoted price exists for the transfer of an **identical or similar** liability/own equity instrument and there is **no identical item held by another entity as an asset** – measure the fair value of the liability or equity instrument using a **valuation technique from the perspective of a market participant** that owes the liability or has issued the equity

Fair Value – IFRS 13

IFRS 13 levels

Level 1   quoted prices in an active market for identical assets or liabilities

Level 2   inputs other than Level 1 that are observable, either directly or indirectly

               e.g. quoted prices for similar assets in active markets or for identical or similar assets in non-active markets or use of quoted interest rates for valuation purposes

Level 3   unobservable inputs for the asset or liability

               e.g. the entity's own assumptions about market exit value

The entity should **maximise** the use of **observable** inputs and **minimise** the use of **unobservable** inputs

Valuation approaches

Income approach	discounted future flows (cash flows, income and expenses)
Market approach	use of prices and other relevant information generated by market transactions involving identical or comparable assets, liabilities or a group of assets and liabilities (such as a business)
Cost approach	the amount that would be required currently to replace the service capacity of an asset (current replacement cost)

The valuation of unlisted equity shares is likely to be particularly challenging and will almost certainly be classified as a Level 3 measurement due to the use of unobservable inputs

Entities may use more than one valuation technique to measure FV in a given situation – a change of valuation technique is considered to be a change of accounting estimate in accordance with IAS 8 and must be disclosed in the financial statements

An asset-based approach would be more relevant to a property business whilst an income approach would be more relevant to a service business

Examples of inputs used to measure FV

Level 1	Equity shares (listed)	Market price (unadjusted quoted price)
Level 2	Licensing arrangement	Royalty rate in contract
	CGU	Valuation multiple from comparable businesses
	Inventory	Comparable items, adjusted for relevant differences
	Building	Price per square metre from observable market data
Level 3	CGU	Forecast from entity's own data
	Share option (other than employee-held)	Volatility and related valuation model
	Interest rate swap	Adjustment to mid-market consensus valuation using data not directly observable or as corroborated by observable market data

Financial instruments – convertible bonds

Suggested mark allocation in an FR question (CR Q2): 6 marks

A convertible bond is a compound instrument per IAS 32 – the equity and liability components should be separated

The liability component at inception is calculated as the present value of future cash flows (capital and interest) from the instrument, discounted by a market interest rate for an instrument with the same terms and conditions **except for** the ability to convert to shares

Note – do **not** use the **coupon** rate involved in the instrument for the discounting – use a **market rate** for an equivalent instrument without the conversion option

The **equity** component is the **residual** amount i.e. the difference between the calculated liability and the consideration paid for the bond

Pro forma – example of a £20m loan at 5% with a discount factor of 7% (rate applicable to a similar instrument without the conversion option)

	Cash flow at 5%	Discount at 7%	£000
31 Dec 2015	1,000	$1/1.07$	935
31 Dec 2016	1,000	$1/1.07^2$	873
31 Dec 2017	1,000	$1/1.07^3$	816
31 Dec 2018	1,000*	$1/1.07^4$	763
	20,000*	$1/1.07^4$	15,258
Total liability			18,645
Equity (balance)			1,355
Consideration			20,000

The cash flow is calculated by multiplying the consideration by the applicable coupon interest rate i.e. the rate applying to the loan. These figures are all based on amounts **before** you do the split accounting.

*As the capital repayment and final year of interest are discounted by the same discount factor, you may wish to do the final 2 rows above as a single calculation to save time (i.e. 21,000 at $1/1.07^4$)

Note that it is possible to use an **annuity factor** for the **interest** cash flows as these are the same each year – this may save time if you have an instrument that lasts for a few years

However, if you use an **annuity factor** for the **interest** cash flows, do not forget to also have a **separate discount factor** calculation for the large **capital** repayment in the final year

Treatment of transaction costs

The total transaction costs should be split **pro rata** between the liability and equity components based on the pro forma calculation above i.e. you must find the PV of the liability and the residual equity amount before allocating the transaction costs – do not forget to **reduce** the value of the **liability** and the **equity** component by the allocated transaction costs

Financial instruments – IFRS 9

Note – please check our disclaimer stated on **page 12** of this book for an explanation of how the notes in this section have been compiled

Interaction with IFRS 7 and IAS 32

Any instrument falling under IFRS 9 should be adequately presented and disclosed in accordance with IFRS 7 and IAS 32

Qualitative and quantitative disclosures under IFRS 7 will need to be made regarding the entity's exposure to risk

There should also be disclosure of the carrying amount of assets and liabilities by IFRS 9 category

There should be disclosure of any interest recognised in profit or loss

Financial assets under IFRS 9

The 3 categories of financial assets under IFRS 9

1. Amortised cost – objective is to hold the asset to **collect contractual cash flows** and contractual terms give rise on specified dates to cash flows that are **solely** payments of principal and interest on the principal outstanding

2. Fair value through OCI (FVtOCI) – held within a business model whose objective is achieved by **both collecting contractual cash flows and selling financial assets** and contractual terms give rise on specified dates to cash flows that are **solely** payments of principal and interest on the principal outstanding

3. Fair value through profit or loss (FVtPL) – all assets that are not treated as held at either amortised cost or FVtOCI – derivatives should always be treated as FVtPL unless part of a hedging arrangement

Equity instruments – irrevocable election to treat as FVtOCI

Equity instruments may not be classified as measured at amortised cost and must be measured at fair value – if an equity instrument is not held for trading, an entity can make an irrevocable election at initial recognition to measure the instrument at FVtOCI with only **dividend** income being recognised in profit or loss

Business model

The IFRS 9 asset categorisation is made on the basis of both the entity's business model for managing the financial asset and the contractual cost flow characteristics of the financial asset

Assessment of the business model is not made at the individual financial instrument level

The assessment is made based on how key management personnel actually manage the business rather than the intentions of management for specific financial assets

Financial instruments – IFRS 9

The entity can have more than one different business model for different portfolios of assets – for example, some assets could be held to collect contractual cash flows whilst other assets of the same type could be held with the objective of trading to realise changes in fair value

If the entity wishes to apply a business model involving the holding of assets to collect cash flows, it is not necessary to hold all assets to maturity – this model can apply even if sales of financial assets of the relevant type occur

Derecognition of a financial asset

Derecognition should take place when the **contractual rights** to the cash flows from the financial asset **expire** or the entity transfers **substantially all of the risks and rewards of ownership** of the financial asset to another party

FVtOCI categorisation for equity investments

Under IFRS 9, all equity instruments should be measured at fair value in the SFP with value changes recognised in the P&L except for those equity investments for which the entity has elected to present value changes in OCI

The FVtOCI categorisation is only appropriate if:

- the equity investment is not held for trading

- the entity has made an irrevocable election at initial recognition to measure it at FVtOCI with only dividend income recognised in profit or loss

Financial assets at FVtOCI should initially be measured at fair value – at the end of each reporting period, such a financial asset should be remeasured to fair value with any changes recognised in OCI

Treatment of transaction costs

IFRS 9 states that (unless the financial asset is measured at FVtPL) the transaction costs are added to the value of the asset rather than being written off to the P&L

Zero interest loan issued at par

IFRS 9 requires a financial asset to be measured initially at fair value

A zero interest rate loan issued at par would not result in an arm's-length transaction and IFRS 9 requires the fair value in such a case to be determined as the present value of the cash receipts under the effective interest rate method

The discount rate should be the rate that applies on similar loans which carry an interest rate

The entity will then need to consider the business model involved in holding the asset to determine its subsequent treatment

It may be appropriate to use the amortised cost method as a loan is a non-derivative financial asset with a determinable repayment date and the entity may have an intention to hold the investment to maturity rather than to realise gains through sale (obviously, please check the question Exhibit content here carefully)

Financial instruments – IFRS 9

In this case, there would need to be an unwinding of any discount each year which will be treated as finance income

Investments in other companies which are less significant than an associate

Such an investment is insignificant in terms of group accounting and is therefore governed by IAS 32/IFRS 9

Loans to employees

IFRS 9 requires financial assets (except those at FVtPL or FVtOCI) to be measured on initial recognition at fair value plus transaction costs

Usually the fair value of the consideration given represents the fair value of the asset – however, this is not necessarily the case with an interest-free loan

An interest-free loan to an employee is not costless to the employer and the face value may not be the same as the fair value

To arrive at the fair value, the entity needs to consider other market transactions in the same instrument, discounting the face value of the loan based on interest rates for an equivalent instrument

The difference between the face value of the loan and the discounted figure is the extra cost to the employer of not charging a market rate of interest

This should be treated as employee compensation under IAS 19 and therefore charged over the period of the loan to the P&L each year

To measure the loan at amortised cost under IFRS 9, the following criteria must be met:

> (1) business model test. The objective of the entity's business model is to hold the financial asset to collect the contractual cash flows (rather than to sell the instrument prior to its contractual maturity to realise its fair value changes)

> (2) cash flow characteristics test. The contractual terms of the financial asset give rise on specified dates to cash flows that are solely payments of principal and interest on the principal outstanding

If the criteria are satisfied, the loan should be measured at amortised cost using the effective interest method – the effective interest rate will be the same rate as used to discount the loan to present value so apply this rate to calculate the finance cost in the P&L for the year i.e. unwind the discount

Costs of issuing debt or equity – interaction with IFRS 3

IFRS 3 requires that the costs of issuing debt or equity are accounted for under the rules of IFRS 9

Joint venture in the individual financial statements of the parent company

In a parent company's separate financial statements, such an investment will be held in accordance with IAS 27 (2011), namely:

> at cost

Financial instruments – IFRS 9

in accordance with IFRS 9

using the equity method specified in IAS 28

Financial liabilities under IFRS 9

Amortised cost debenture issued by the entity (liability)

Under IFRS 9, an issued debenture should initially be measured in the financial statements at the fair value of the consideration received net of issue costs – the exception to this is where the financial instrument is designated as at FVtPL

The debenture should then be measured at amortised cost using the effective interest method – the amount recognised in profit or loss as an interest cost should be based on the effective interest rate and not the coupon rate – any difference between the actual interest paid as cash (based on the coupon rate) and interest charged (based on the effective interest rate) would represent a proportion of any premium or discount on the debenture so that this is recognised gradually on an accruals basis rather than purely at the date of redemption

Financial liability where part of the gain or loss relates to an entity's own creditworthiness

IFRS 9 requires that financial liabilities which are designated as measured at FVtPL are treated differently where part of the gain or loss relates to an entity's own creditworthiness

In this case, the gain or loss in the period must be classified into:

gain or loss resulting from credit risk, and

any other gain or loss

This provision of IFRS 9 was in response to an anomaly in IAS 39 regarding changes in the credit risk of a financial liability – under this anomaly, if there were no separate treatment of the gain or loss resulting from credit risk, then when an entity's creditworthiness deteriorates and the fair value of its issued debt (a liability for the entity) decreases then the entity would recognise a gain as a result of the decline in its own creditworthiness – this is counterintuitive

IFRS 9 requires the gain or loss as a result of credit risk to be recognised in OCI unless it creates or enlarges an accounting mismatch, in which case it is recognised in profit or loss

The other element of the gain or loss (unrelated to the result of credit risk) is recognised in profit or loss

On derecognition, any gains or losses recognised in OCI as a result of this special rule are not transferred to profit or loss, although the cumulative gain or loss may be transferred within equity

Derecognition of a financial liability

Under IFRS 9, an entity should derecognise a financial liability when it is extinguished i.e. when the obligation specified in the contract is discharged or cancelled or expires

An entity discharges its obligation by paying in cash, other financial assets or by delivering other goods or services to the counterparty

Financial instruments – IFRS 9

When a liability is extinguished, the difference between its carrying amount and the consideration paid (including any non-cash assets transferred and any new liabilities assumed) is recognised in profit or loss

Loan arrangement fee regarding a loan taken on by an entity (liability)

Under IFRS 9, a loan arrangement fee should not be treated as an administrative expense

Instead, such a fee should have been deducted from the loan balance outstanding and charged over the loan period in proportion to the outstanding balance on the loan

Sale and leaseback which is not a sale under IFRS 15

Where a transfer is not in substance a sale under IFRS 15, the seller-lessee accounts for the proceeds as a financial liability in accordance with IFRS 9

Financial instruments – impairment – IFRS 9

Note – please check our disclaimer stated on **page 12** of this book for an explanation of how the notes in this section have been compiled

General approach to impairment under IFRS 9

IFRS 9 is based on the premise of providing for **expected** losses

The financial statements should reflect the general pattern of deterioration or improvement in the credit quality of financial instruments within the scope of IFRS 9

Expected credit losses are the expected shortfall in contractual cash flows, defined in IFRS 9 as the weighted average of credit losses with the respective risks of a default occurring as the weights

On initial recognition, an entity must create a credit loss allowance/provision equal to the 12-month expected credit losses – this is calculated by multiplying the probability of default occurring in the next 12 months by the total lifetime expected credit losses that would result from that default

IFRS 9 requires that, if credit risk increases significantly since initial recognition, the 12-month expected credit losses amount should be replaced by lifetime expected credit losses

Lifetime expected credit losses are defined as the expected credit losses that result from all possible default events over the expected life of a financial instrument

There is a rebuttable presumption that lifetime expected losses should be provided for if contractual cash flows are more than 30 days overdue

IFRS 9 allows a simplified approach to the expected loss model in respect of trade receivables which do not have an IFRS 15 financing element

In this case, the loss allowance is measured at the lifetime expected credit losses immediately from initial recognition

> Should a receivable exceed the credit limit then it is likely that the allowance established based on expected credit losses at initial recognition should be increased

A receivable is a financial instrument and is therefore subject to IFRS 9 and scoped out of IAS 37

3 stage approach to loss allowances under IFRS 9

Under the full 3 stage approach, the 12-month expected credit losses are calculated by multiplying the probability of default in the next 12 months by the lifetime expected credit losses that would result from the default

The 3 stages in the IFRS expected credit loss model are:

> Stage 1 – initial recognition (and subsequently if no significant deterioration in credit risk): 12-month expected credit losses recognised and interest calculated on the gross carrying amount

> Stage 2 – credit risk increases significantly (rebuttable presumption if more than 30 days past due): lifetime expected credit losses recognised with interest calculated on the gross carrying amount

Financial instruments – impairment – IFRS 9

Stage 3 – objective evidence of impairment exists at the reporting date: lifetime expected credit losses recognised with interest calculated on the net carrying amount net of the allowance for credit losses after the date that evidence exists

A simplified approach is permitted for trade receivables, contract assets and lease receivables – for trade receivables or contract assets that do not have an IFRS 15 financing element, the loss allowance is measured at the lifetime expected credit losses, immediately from initial recognition

Provided that the receivables do not have an IFRS 15 financing element, it is legitimate to adopt this simplified approach

A receivable is a financial instrument and is therefore subject to IFRS 9 and scoped out of IAS 37

Investment in loan stock which is impaired at initial recognition

The entity should follow the IFRS 9 "expected loss" method – credit losses are recognised when expected rather than when incurred

On initial recognition, the entity should recognise the 12-month expected credit losses by multiplying the value of the loan stock by the percentage probability that the borrower will default on the loan with a 100% loss

An impairment loss on a financial asset at amortised cost requires a corresponding entry to an allowance account, which is offset against the carrying amount of the financial asset in the SFP and results in an impairment charge in the P&L for the year

At the year-end, expected credit losses are reassessed and the percentage probability may be adjusted accordingly – if there is now a lower percentage probability of a 100% default, the impairment allowance may need to be reduced

There may also be a finance cost, being the unwinding of the discount on the allowance at initial recognition

> You may be given an opening allowance in the question wording so look out for the relevant discount rate to apply – this may not necessarily be stated right next to the opening allowance figure so you may need to look around for the necessary rate

To take account of the unwinding of the discount and the fact that the year-end impairment allowance may be changed due to a change in the estimated percentage probability of default, you may need to insert an increase or decrease in the allowance as a balancing finance cost or finance income, using a tabular format

For example, if the opening impairment allowance was 150 and the closing allowance needs to be 60 with an unwinding of discount equal to 12 then you would need to put together a table to find the balancing amount (in this case, finance income due to the overall decrease in the allowance required):

Opening allowance	150
Finance cost (unwinding of discount)	12
Finance income (decrease in allowance) – balancing figure	(102)
Closing allowance	60

The closing allowance of 60 is then deducted from the carrying amount of the bond at the year end

Risk of non-payment on a receivable

A receivable is a financial instrument and is therefore subject to IFRS 9 and scoped out of IAS 37

© ACA Simplified 2019. No copying or reproduction permitted.

Financial instruments – impairment – IFRS 9

IFRS 9 takes account of the relevant percentage risk that the customer will default – however, if there is a 5% risk that the customer will default this does not mean that the entity should simply take 5% of the related revenue figure and treat this as a receivables expense

Instead, IFRS 9 uses an expected credit loss method

In the case of trade receivables which do not have an IFRS 15 financing element, IFRS 9 allows a simplified approach to the expected credit loss method – the loss allowance is measured at the lifetime expected credit losses, from initial recognition – alternatively, the entity could instead follow the usual and full 3 stage approach of IFRS 9

Under the simplified approach, this amount may in practice be calculated as the relevant percentage risk multiplied by the related receivables figure i.e. if there is a 5% risk of default then apply 5% to the related revenue figure but this is recognised as an "expected credit loss", rather than as a receivables expense – and this is only possible in relation to trade receivables that do not have an IFRS 15 financing element

Remember to add an amount to reflect the unwinding of discount during the year (using the discount rate information provided in the question Exhibit material) – this interest will be recognised in the P&L and will increase the loss allowance by the same amount

Forex translation – single entity accounts

Suggested mark allocation in an FR question (CR Q2): 2 marks per transaction

(Please note that this topic covers currency recognition rules for a single company rather than the consolidation of an overseas subsidiary into the group accounts – for the more complex issue of consolidation of an overseas subsidiary please see the section starting on **page 84**.)

IAS 21 requires amounts to be translated into the entity's "functional currency"

The **functional currency** is "the currency of the primary economic environment in which the entity operates"

The **primary economic environment** "is normally the one in which it primarily generates and expends cash"

Translation rules – single entity accounts (see exceptions in the next section)

Initial recognition – use the **spot rate** on the date of the transaction – an average rate may be used if exchange rates do not fluctuate significantly

Monetary items – use the **closing rate**

Non-monetary items carried at **historical cost** – use the exchange rate at the date of the transaction (historic rate)

Non-monetary items carried at FV – use the exchange rate that existed **when the value was measured (closing rate)**

Exchange differences should be recognised such as to match the underlying transaction – exchange differences on monetary items should be recognised in the P&L – exchange differences on non-monetary items recognised in OCI should also be recognised through OCI

Exceptions to the general rules

A monetary item designed as a hedge of a net investment – any exchange difference that forms part of the gain or loss on the hedging instrument is recognised as **OCI**

A monetary item designated as a hedging instrument in a cash flow hedge – any exchange difference that forms part of the gain or loss on the hedging instrument is recognised as **OCI**

Exchange differences arising in respect of monetary items which are part of the net investment are recognised in profit or loss in the individual financial statements – however, in the CSFP the exchange differences are recognised **through OCI and within equity**

Normally non-monetary items are not retranslated at the year-end in the individual entity accounts so no exchange differences arise – however, note the following exceptions:

> When a gain or loss on a non-monetary item is recognised in OCI (e.g. revaluation of a property denominated in a foreign currency) then any related exchange differences should be recognised as OCI

Forex translation – single entity accounts

When a gain or loss on a non-monetary item is recognised in profit or loss, any exchange component of that gain or loss is also recognised in profit or loss

Remember that in the impairment testing of foreign currency non-monetary assets, the carrying amount should be reset to the lower of the carrying amount translated at the exchange rate at the date when that amount was determined (i.e. an historic rate at a past date) and the recoverable amount, translated at the exchange rate at the date when that value was determined (e.g. the **closing rate** at the reporting date)

Inventories

Inventories are a **non-monetary** asset – the inventory (and associated liability if not yet paid in cash) are recorded at the spot rate on the day of purchase

The inventories need no further translating – any **liability** to pay for the inventories, however, **is** a **monetary** item and should be translated at the reporting date using the **closing rate** with exchange gains and losses being taken to **profit or loss**

Inventories must be valued at the **lower** of cost and net realisable value

Going Concern

Suggested mark allocation in an FR question (CR Q2): 2 marks

Duties of management and disclosures

Directors are **required** to report that the business is a going concern, with assumptions or qualifications if necessary – if the company has a full listing then this will be part of their responsibilities under the **UK Corporate Governance Code**

If there is adequate **disclosure** in the financial statements by the directors regarding the uncertainties of the going concern assumption then an **unmodified** audit opinion with an **emphasis of matter** paragraph is likely to be sufficient

If the directors **do not disclose** going concern uncertainties appropriately then it may be necessary to **modify** the audit opinion

Duties of auditors

Discuss with management and perform other audit tests

Government Grants

Suggested mark allocation in an FR question (CR Q2): 6 marks

Recognition

Recognition of a government grant should occur when there is reasonable assurance that

> the entity will comply with the relevant conditions and
>
> the entity will receive the grant

Note that in some cases the second criterion will be fulfilled automatically as the money will already have been received – you will therefore only have to assess the first criterion based on the **probability** of fulfilment of conditions

Make sure you apply these points to the scenario by checking if the conditions have been complied with (referencing the relevant facts in your answer)

The likely mistake made by the client is to use a cash basis rather than an accruals basis to recognise the grant

Capital grants

There are 2 methods of recognition – these are both designed to ensure that the grant hits the P&L at the same time/rate as the underlying item on which a grant has been given

Note that both methods give the same net P&L impact so there is no "favourable" approach (although the impact on certain ratios may be different)

Netting off method

Deduct the amount of the grant from the cost of the asset – this will reduce the amount which is depreciated, reducing the depreciation charge

> However, it will also reduce the value of assets, which could impact on ratios

Deferred income method

Set up the grant as deferred income in the SFP – release this to the P&L on a systematic and rational basis over the useful life of the asset (normally this would correspond to the method of depreciation on the related asset)

> This will leave the asset value at a higher amount, impacting ratios – however, the deferred income will increase liabilities

Income grants

e.g. grants to employ local employees over a 3 year period

Such a grant should be recognised over the same period as the underlying item i.e. 3 years in the example here

Government Grants

The grant should not be recognised unless there is reasonable assurance that the entity will comply with any **conditions** attached to the grant and that the **grant will be received**

Note that in some cases the second criterion will be fulfilled automatically as the money will already have been received – you will therefore only have to assess the first criterion based on the **probability** of fulfilment of conditions

It is likely that the client will have recognised the **cash** received as the P&L entry – this is incorrect – you will therefore have to set up a **deferred income** account as some revenue may not be recognised yet

The grant should **not** be recognised as **revenue** – it could either be shown as other income in the P&L or it could be netted off against the expenditure to which it relates e.g. as part of operating costs

Make sure you split the deferred income account into current and non-current elements

As it is likely that you will have some **time apportionment** the current year, it is easiest to first calculate a full year of revenue as you can use this instantly as the current element of the deferred income account – then time apportion this full year figure as appropriate for the current year to provide the P&L amount – the remainder must be the non-current element of deferred income

Summary of technique

1. Calculate a full year of deferred income – current liability

2. Time apportion the above figure from step 1 as required – current year P&L income

3. The remaining balance (i.e. the total grant figure minus figures from step 1 in step 2) is the non-current liability

Repayment of government grants

If a grant becomes repayable then this should be accounted for as a change in accounting estimate

Repayment of an income grant

This should be first set against any unamortised deferred credit set up in respect of the grant – to the extent that repayment exceeds any such deferred credit or where no deferred credit exists then the repayment should be recognised immediately as an expense

Repayment of a capital grant

This should be recognised either by increasing the carrying amount of the asset or reducing the deferred income balance by the amount repayable

The cumulative additional depreciation that would have been recognised to date as an expense in the absence of the grant should be recognised immediately as an expense

Disclosures

Accounting policy adopted for government grants, including the methods of presentation

Nature and extent of government grants recognised in the financial statements

Indication of other forms of government assistance from which the entity has directly benefited

Unfilled conditions and other contingencies attaching to government assistance that have been recognised

Groups – acquisitions

Suggested mark allocation in an FR question (CR Q2): 7-8 marks

Tip

Do not forget to talk about the NCI!

We have provided several further Group sections on the following pages so please do make use of these

Loss-making subsidiary – in this case, there will probably be a mark for suggesting that an impairment review is needed even in the year of acquisition

Treatment

Consolidation should occur if there is "**control**" over the subsidiary

A **majority shareholding** i.e. greater than 50% would **normally** indicate control – however, other factors may be relevant under IFRS 10 (see next page)

Issues to consider

Measure consideration at FV

Transaction costs such as professional fees should not form part of the consideration and should instead be recognised directly in profit or loss

> An exception (rarely tested) is that the costs of arranging financial liabilities (e.g. loans) and issuing equity are deducted from the liability/equity

Intangible assets should be recognised separately if they arise from legal or other contractual rights – these assets do not form part of goodwill – they should be amortised – there will be an NCI impact

Goodwill should be reviewed annually for impairment

Gain on a bargain purchase (negative goodwill)

Here the value of assets acquired exceeds the consideration paid

Reassess the identification and measurement of the net assets and the measurement of the consideration

If the amounts are correct then the gain on bargain purchase should be recognised as part of profit or loss for the period

Tip – do not forget to mention the NCI impact of your adjustments – easy additional marks on a follow through approach for a relatively simple calculation

We have provided several further Group sections on the following pages so please do make use of these

Assessing control under IFRS 10 – advanced points

Note – only include these points if the matter of control appears complicated in the scenario – in most group answers, you would not need the below details

IFRS 10 states that an investor controls an investee if and only if it has all the following

> power over the investee
>
> exposure, or rights, to variable returns from its involvement with the investee
>
> the ability to use its power over the investee to affect the amount of the investor's returns

The fact that board members may not have actually exercised control in practice is not a determining factor in deciding whether the entity has control over the investee

We also need to consider powers to appoint board members – if there are such appointment powers for board members other than the entity which has a majority shareholding, then the matter may not be so straightforward and the shareholding greater than 50% may not be sufficient to create "control"

In some cases, control of board decisions over a fundamental aspect of the company such as R&D or Finance e.g. if the owner can appoint a specific Director to be the head of R&D or Finance could also confer control if that division is fundamental to the investee

The right to acquire further shares through a call option could also be relevant – IFRS 10 requires an investor to consider potential voting rights in considering whether it has control and whether the right is substantive i.e. whether the holder has the practical ability to exercise the right

If "control" is not held, the investment cannot be recognised as a subsidiary and would be recognised instead as an associate

Groups – associates

Suggested mark allocation in an FR question (CR Q2): 3 marks

A holding of 20% or more of the voting power in an investee is presumed to provide significant influence and create an associate position – however, the 20% figure is rebuttable and an associate could exist with more or less than this amount depending on whether the facts indicate that significant influence exists through one or more of the following

- representation on the board of directors or participation in policy making decisions
- material transactions between the investor and investee
- interchange of managerial personnel
- provision of essential technical information

Equity method of accounting

Recognise initially at cost – increase or decrease by the investor's share in the post-acquisition change in the associate's net assets (profits or losses)

Cost	X
Share of post-acquisition change in net assets	X
Less investor's **share** of dividends paid by associate	(X)
Less impairment losses to date	(X)
	X

The investor's share in profits/losses should be recognised in the investor's CSPL net of any impairment loss

Eliminate profits and losses on transactions between the investor and associate to the extent of the investor's share

The investor's interest can only be written below nil (creating a liability) if the investor has incurred obligations on behalf of the associate

There is **no line by line addition** of items in the SFP – instead there is a single line under non-current assets

No goodwill calculation is performed

The whole interest is subject to an **impairment review** if there is an objective **indicator of impairment**

Trading transactions should not be cancelled on consolidation – the associate is not part of the group

- No adjustment to revenue or CoS in the CSPL
- Receivables and payables due to/from the associate should be carried across into the CSFP

Unrealised profits should be eliminated, but only to the extent of the investor's share – the adjustment is made in the books of the seller

- This applies to both the transfer of goods and the transfer of non-current assets

Groups – associate to subsidiary

Suggested mark allocation in an FR question (CR Q2): 7-8 marks

Key points to mention

Refer to the fact that control has been achieved – goodwill arises on the transaction and an NCI will be created in relation to the percentage owned by minority shareholders

Treatment

Continue to treat the entity as an associate right up to the date when control is achieved – therefore continue to apply the equity method and credit or debit the statement of profit or loss with a time apportioned amount of profit or loss e.g. £5m x 4 / 12 x 30%

> If this is a profit, the debit would increase the investment in associate balance in the SFP

State that for the remaining months of the year after control is achieved, the entity should be consolidated using the acquisition method and assets, liabilities, income and expenses should be fully consolidated in

Consider whether there is an NCI – if the entity is now 100% owned, state that there are no entries in respect of NCI – if the entity is now, say 80% owned, then state that the NCI will hold 20% of assets and will take 20% of profit or loss for the period after control is achieved

Calculate the gain on the increase in stake (in the exam, it is highly likely that the entity will record a gain and not a loss here) using the following pro forma

Original cost	X
Cumulative share of profit or loss to the end of the previous period	X
Share of profit or loss for the current period to the date control is achieved	X*
Carrying amount at time of change in status	X**

*this figure should be the same amount that you calculated above when indicating the amount of profit or loss to take **before** control is achieved

**State that IFRS 3 requires this carrying amount to be restated to fair value – hence compare the total of the above pro-forma calculation with the FV of the shares given in the question – if the FV is higher than the carrying amount calculated above, a gain occurs

In an exam scenario, it is likely that there will be a **gain** as the FV of the shares is normally higher than the carrying amount in the above pro forma – state that this gain is recognised in **profit or loss for the year**, most likely within "other operating income"

Goodwill calculation

As well as calculating the gain on sale as a result of updating to FV (see above) you will need to calculate goodwill as normal as a subsidiary has been acquired

The only real difference is that you need to include the **FV of the shares already held** in **addition** to the normal inclusion of **consideration** – in other words at the top of the pro forma you should have the **consideration** (as normal) **plus the FV of the shares already held** when transforming the associate into

Groups – associate to subsidiary

a subsidiary (different to the normal calculation) – see below for an explanation of how to separately calculate any gain or loss on the FV of shares already held

The rest of the goodwill calculation is as normal – do not forget to mention that the goodwill should not be amortised but should be reviewed for impairment on an annual basis (and earlier if there is any specific indicator of impairment)

Previous investment – shares already held

Any gain or loss on derecognition of the existing shareholding is recognised in the P&L unless the equity interest previously held was subject to an irrevocable election to hold the investment at fair value through OCI (in which case the gain or loss is taken to OCI or, in the SFP, to other components of equity)

→ FV of previously held equity interest at acq   X
  less: Investment CA at acq   (X)
                                          Profit/loss to P/L

Groups – disposal of a subsidiary

Suggested mark allocation in an FR question (CR Q2): 6 marks

Complete disposal

Overview of the complete disposal calculation

Effectively, you are comparing the proceeds received against the value of the subsidiary which the entity holds (net assets less the NCI plus remaining goodwill after impairment)

Rather than trying to calculate all of this in one big calculation as the Study Manual and past papers try to do, we would recommend that you split the calculation into 3 parts:

1. Remaining value of goodwill – goodwill at acquisition less impairments to date

2. Carrying amount of net assets based disposal – net assets at the prior year end plus or minus profit or loss for the current year (look out the time apportionment here)

3. NCI in net assets at the date of disposal – this may be tricky but just make an attempt and take the follow-through marks

After calculating the 3 elements, you can put together a final working as

Proceeds	X
plus NCI at disposal	X
less total subsidiary net assets at disposal	(X)
less goodwill at disposal	(X)
Profit or loss on disposal	X/(X)

(NCI is added back to ensure that on a net basis only the parent's share of the subsidiary's net assets is being disposed of)

The profit or loss on disposal should be recognised in the CSPL under discontinued operations

The results for the subsidiary up to the date of disposal should be included in the CSPL

The parent no longer controls any of the assets or liabilities of the subsidiary after sale so mention that the CSFP should not recognise any of the subsidiary's assets or liabilities

The NCI should include the NCI share of the results of the subsidiary up to the date of disposal (look out for time apportionment here) – on disposal, the CSoCIE should have the remaining NCI deducted to clear out the NCI after disposal

Tip – consider IFRS 5

If the investment in the subsidiary represented a separate major line of business of the group, the results of the subsidiary for the year should be presented separately in accordance with IFRS 5

Groups – disposal of a subsidiary

A single net figure for the profit or loss for the discontinued operation should be disclosed on the face of the CSPL – this is made up of the profit or loss on disposal and the profit or loss for the period to the date of disposal

A disclosure note should show the breakdown of this figure into revenue, costs and profit on disposal

The prior period results should be reclassified as discontinued in order to ensure comparability

Groups – forex consolidation

Suggested mark allocation in an FR question (CR Q2): 20 marks if no other elements of the question – 8 marks if only a "mini consolidation" is required i.e. there are several other FR points in the question

Note that there will be plenty of marks allocated to **explaining the principles** behind the adjustments – you must include **some narrative** and not just the numbers

Important note

We strongly recommend that you take in a copy of a past paper or Question Bank example of a full forex consolidation, annotated with your own reminders and notes – this will be helpful to follow the process through

This section only provides reminders of how to perform the process – it does not provide a fully worked-through example and we do not know what particular areas you find difficult so please do create your own personally-annotated example and bring this into the examination with you.

Treatment

Functional currency

This is the currency of the primary **economic operations** of the entity

Presentation currency

This is the currency in which the financial statements are **presented**

The presentation currency of the parent of the group is likely to be the same as the functional currency

Overview of the forex consolidation process (see next pages for the details of each step)

The financial statements of subsidiaries with a functional currency other than the presentation currency of the parent must be translated on consolidation.

1. Translate **assets** and **liabilities** at the **closing** rate at the year end

2. Translate **equity** on acquisition at **either** the exchange rate **at acquisition** or the **closing** rate

(Per the Study Manual, no guidance is provided in IAS 21 as to how amounts in equity should be translated – therefore **either** approach is permissible although an entity should follow a **consistent** policy between periods)

3. Translate **income** and **expenses** at the **average** rate for the year

Previously the financial statements balanced but now you have (correctly) started using different exchange rates so an imbalance necessarily occurs – therefore:

4. Present in a **separate component** of equity the exchange differences which inevitably arise from application of the above rules – these **exchange differences** are reported through OCI rather than the P&L

Groups – forex consolidation

5. Treat **goodwill** as an **asset** of the relevant subsidiary and translate at the **closing rate**

6. Eliminate **intragroup** balances and transactions as **normal** on consolidation

Steps 1 & 2 – Translation of SFP

Translate assets and liabilities at the **closing** rate

Translate **equity** and **pre-acquisition** retained earnings at the rate applicable on acquisition or at the closing rate (the Study Manual states that either method is acceptable, provided that it is applied consistently from one period to the next)

Translate **post-acquisition** retained earnings at the **average** rates for the current year

To make the statements balance, set up a **translation reserve** as necessary and record this immediately below retained earnings in the SFP

> You can enter this simply as a balancing figure but ideally it should match the amount calculated in the **Translation reserve in the SFP section** below – try to use the result of that below calculation if possible because it is simpler than getting all the above changes correct

Step 3 – Translation of SPLOCI

Translate all amounts at the **average** rate for the year

As all amounts are translated at the **same** rate, there is **no need for any translation reserve** for the P&L

However, there may of course be some exchange gains and losses on items such as **loans** or **intra-company purchases** as a result of fluctuating exchange rates during the year – these are included in the SPLOCI and are translated at the average rate as with any other items in the SPLOCI

The point is that you do not need to set up a special "consolidation only" item in relation to the consolidation process of the P&L and OCI (unlike with the SFP and goodwill)

Step 4 – Translation reserve in the SFP (confirmation of subsidiary translation reserve and creation of Consolidated translation reserve)

1. Translate **opening** net assets at the **closing** rate and compare these with **opening** net assets at the **opening** rate

2. Translate profits at the **closing** rate and compare these with profits at the **average** rate

Pro forma

Opening net assets at opening rate

Opening net assets at closing rate

	X

Profit/loss at the average rate

Profit/loss at the closing rate

	X
Exchange gain or loss (net of above 2 totals)	X

3. The net impact of the above 2 translations may lead to a gain or loss – this amount is included as the **translation reserve** of the **subsidiary** and should be the same figure as the translation reserve created as a balancing figure when translating the subsidiary's SFP (see previous page)

> We would recommend that you use the figure based on the working above to put into your SFP rather than simply using a balancing amount as discussed on the previous page because then you should get the relevant marks for this part of the Translation reserve – if you just use a balancing approach, an error in another area of the SFP will mean that you lose this mark as well

4. Allocate the above net gain or net loss to the **group** based on its ownership percentage – allocate the balance to the NCI

5. Finally add or deduct the exchange gain or loss on re-translation of **goodwill** (see below)

6. Add together the group share of the net gain or net loss from step 4 to the gain or loss on retranslation of goodwill from step 5 – this figure is included in the **Consolidated SFP** as a **translation reserve** and is recognised through OCI, not through the P&L

Step 5 – Translation of goodwill

Set up the normal pro forma to calculate goodwill, including consideration transferred as compared to the FV of net assets acquired

Remember to split this between the group and NCI

Translate these amounts at the exchange rate applicable at the **date of acquisition**

Allocate any impairment losses, remembering to split these between the group and NCI – translate the **impairment loss** at the rate applicable at the date of determination of the impairment (in most model answers, this is the **closing rate** i.e. the date of the annual year end impairment test)

Translate the year-end figures after impairment at the **closing rate**

As a result of applying different exchange rates within the pro forma you will need to set up a **foreign exchange gain or loss** to force the figures to agree to back to the value of the goodwill at the year-end as translated into domestic currency at the closing rate

Groups – forex consolidation

Translation reserve and impact on the CSPLOCI

Opening and closing net assets and profits should be translated based on the same principles as above for the SFP

1. Translate opening net assets at the closing rate and compare these with opening net assets at the opening rate

2. Translate profits at the closing rate and compare this with profits at the average rate

The net impact of the above 2 translations may lead to a gain or loss

This amount forms part of the Exchange differences on translating foreign operations through OCI in the CSPLOCI – note that the NCI should take its share of this as part of the NCI figure in the CSPLOCI

The gain or loss on retranslation of goodwill forms the second part of the Exchange differences on translating foreign operations under OCI in the CSPLOCI – this is calculated as above

Set up the normal pro forma to calculate goodwill, including consideration transferred as compared to the FV of net assets acquired

Remember to split this between the group and NCI

Translate these amounts at the exchange rate applicable at the **date of acquisition**

Allocate any **impairment losses**, remembering to split these between the group and NCI – translate the impairment losses at the **closing rate** at the year end

Translate the goodwill figure **after** impairment at the **closing rate** at the year end

As a result of applying 2 different exchange rates in the pro forma (acquisition rate in the top-half of the pro forma and closing rate in the bottom half of the pro forma) you will need to set up a foreign exchange gain or loss to **force the figures to agree to the bottom row, based on the closing rate**

Note that the NCI should also take its share of this as part of the NCI figure in the CSPLOCI – this should be recorded at the bottom of the CSPLOCI under the heading of Total comprehensive income attributable to: NCI

Other aspects of a group forex consolidation

Impact of future changes in exchange rates on the CSFP

There will be 2 impacts from movements in exchange rates between SFP dates: firstly, the value of net assets will change and, secondly, profits will be retranslated at different rates (average and closing rate)

The cost of investment is restated each year in the consolidation to allow for movement in exchange rates. This means that goodwill is restated at the year-end as it is deemed to be an asset of the subsidiary and therefore restated just like any asset

Changes will be taken to OCI in the CSPLOCI and so the NCI will take its share of any adjustment

Translation of a foreign currency loan

The **opening amount** should be translated at the rate applicable on the **last day** of the previous accounting period or the **first day** of the current accounting period

© ACA Simplified 2019. No copying or reproduction permitted.

Groups – forex consolidation

Interest for the year carried to the **income statement** should be translated at the **average** rate for the year

Interest paid in **cash** should be translated at the rate applicable on the **date** of that payment (spot rate) – in an exam scenario, this is likely to be the **closing rate**

The balance carried forward at the year-end should be translated at the **closing rate**

As a result of using the various different rates within the above, there will always be an **exchange gain or loss** to consider as a balancing item – make sure you consider carefully whether you are dealing with a liability or an asset to decide if the movement is a gain or loss

Intragroup loan outstanding (net investment in a foreign operation)

The following rules apply to monetary items which are part of the net investment in a foreign operation on consolidation:

If the monetary item is denominated in the functional currency of the **parent** entity, the exchange difference will be recognised in the profit or loss of the foreign **subsidiary**

If the monetary item is denominated in the functional currency of the **subsidiary**, exchange differences will be recognised in the profit or loss of the **parent** entity

If the monetary item is denominated in the functional currency of **either** entity, then on consolidation the exchange difference will be **removed from the CSPL** and will be recognised **through OCI** and recorded in **equity** in the CSFP

If the monetary item is denominated in a **third** currency which is different from either entity's functional currency, the translation difference should be recognised as part of the **profit or loss of the group**

If the foreign operation is subsequently **disposed of**, the **cumulative** exchange differences previously reported as **OCI** and recognised in **equity** should be **reclassified** and therefore included in the **profit or loss on disposal** recognised in the **CSPL**

Groups – goodwill calculation

Suggested mark allocation in an FR question (CR Q2): 5-6 marks

Tip – mention the need for an impairment review!

As soon as you see that a goodwill calculation is required, get ready to mention at the **end** of your answer that an **impairment review** should be carried out on goodwill at **every year end** or earlier if there is an **indicator** of impairment.

Tip – mention the NCI! (unless the entity has a 100% subsidiary)

Since you are performing a goodwill calculation, you are looking at a **group** scenario – therefore bear in mind our usual tip to always mention the **NCI** impact in group questions – if possible, try to calculate the **NCI at the year-end** i.e. the NCI amount used in the goodwill calculation as adjusted for the NCI share of events during the year (full **follow through** marking will apply here so please just try!)

Remember to comment on the **NCI share** of any adjustment in the goodwill calculation if NCI is measured as a **proportion of net assets** – the net assets will **change** as a result of the goodwill re-measurement so the **NCI share** of net assets will also change

Treatment

Always utilise the **FV** of consideration and the **FV** of assets and liabilities – this is the case even if the assets and liabilities would **not normally be carried at FV** in the financial statements

Important – do not forget to make the statement that **goodwill is not amortised** but is rather **tested annually for impairment** – then check the scenario: is there any indication of losses or changes in demand? These could be indicators of impairment

Acquisition-related transaction costs

These are **written off** to profit or loss – they are **not** included in the **consideration** figure

Contingent consideration

This should be measured at **fair value** in the goodwill calculation and a **corresponding liability** should be recognised (and then **unwound**) – remember to **categorise** the liability as **current** or **non-current** as appropriate

Discounting should be applied using the **company's cost of capital** – the discounted sum should be **added** to **consideration** when calculating goodwill

Make sure you refer to the **unwinding** of the **discount** on the liability, stating that this is taken to profit or loss as a **finance cost** and **increases** the **liability** – look out for **time apportionment** here – calculate the year end **liability** after the **unwinding** of the discount

Groups – goodwill calculation

Restructuring and future losses

The acquiring company should **not** recognise as **liabilities** any future **losses** or **other costs** expected to be incurred as a result of the business combination

A **plan** to restructure does **not** create a present obligation as a result of a past event (so it is not a provision) – additionally such a **plan** does not meet the definition of a **contingent liability** either

Recognition of intangible assets in the subsidiary

These may only be **recognised** separately from goodwill if they are **identifiable**

An intangible asset is **identifiable** only if it is **separable** (capable of being separated or divided and sold separately) or it arises from **contractual or other legal rights**

IFRS 3 gives some examples – these include customer lists and customer contracts

For customer lists to be separately recognised they must be **separable** or arise from **contractual or legal rights** – previously unrecognised internally-generated lists **might** be recognised on acquisition of a new subsidiary if they are deemed to be **separable** or arise from **contractual or legal rights**

IFRS 3 states that a customer list acquired in a business combination does **not** meet the criterion of **separability** if the **terms** of **confidentiality** or other **agreements prohibit** the entity from selling, leasing or otherwise exchanging information about its customers

Recognition of contingent liabilities

Normally, under IAS 37, contingent liabilities are not **recognised**, but only **disclosed** – in other words, no monetary value or related calculation regarding the contingent liability is applied within the financial statements and the users are simply given a **narrative explanation** that the contingent liability may exist

In the case of a **business combination**, however, contingent liabilities of the acquired company **are recognised** if the fair value can be measured reliably (it is **not** necessary for the outflow to be **probable**)

After initial recognition as part of the business combination process, the contingent liability should be recognised at the **higher** of the amount that would be recognised under IAS 37 and the amount initially recognised

Adjustments after the initial calculation of goodwill is complete

If **provisional** values have been used, the acquiring entity should retrospectively recognise any **adjustments** to those provisional values if the adjustments become apparent **within 12 months of the acquisition date** i.e. **replacing** the provisional figures with the new figures for the purposes of the goodwill calculation (adjusting the **carrying amount** of assets and **goodwill** as necessary)

Any further adjustment **outside the 12 month** period should only be recognised to correct an **error** rather than an estimate.

If further information in relation to an **estimate** emerges **after** the expiry of the 12 month period, this is **not** taken into account – only **errors** should be so adjusted

Groups – goodwill calculation

Remember to comment on the **NCI share** of any adjustment in the goodwill calculation if NCI is measured as a **proportion of net assets** – the net assets will **change** as a result of the goodwill re-measurement so the NCI share of net assets will also change

Deferred consideration – equity shares

Apply the **FV** of the shares on the date the consideration is recognised (usually the acquisition date)

Deferred consideration – cash

Apply the **FV** of future cash receivable – this is the same as the present value of the cash receivable

Apply a **discount rate** for the relevant number of years before the cash is payable – remember to **start** this from the **date the consideration is recognised/the acquisition date** and **not** from the **end** of the accounting period (unless (unusually) the acquisition occurs on the final day of the accounting period)

As with all discounting, remember to mention that the **unwinding** of the discount will be a finance cost in profit or loss – look out for **time apportionment** here – add this amount to the value of the initial asset to state the **year end carrying amount** of the asset

Deferred tax on goodwill – consolidated goodwill versus purchased goodwill

Tax authorities look at individual financial statements and charge tax on individual entities – they do not recognise goodwill that arises on consolidation as this relates to an asset of a group and the tax authorities do not tax groups as such (only the individual entities within the group)

IAS 12 indicates that **no deferred tax is recognised on goodwill** arising in a business combination (but this does not mean there are no deferred tax implications of a business combination – see our **Deferred tax** notes starting on **page 34**)

Note that the tax authorities may recognise purchased goodwill i.e. where an individual company purchases the assets and liabilities of a target rather than shares – the assets and liabilities are measured at FV and compared to the consideration – the entity may therefore have "purchased goodwill" rather than creating goodwill on consolidation

If the treatment of the "purchased goodwill" is **different** in the **financial statements** compared to the **tax treatment**, then deferred tax could arise

Fair value adjustments

IFRS 3 requires all assets and liabilities to be re-measured at **fair value** – this will override the carrying amount used in the accounts

Remember that for consolidation purposes you should depreciate the assets based on this **higher** fair value – try to state the **additional** depreciation that this will cause, and look out for **time apportionment** – remember to mention that this will **reduce profits** for the year

(In exam papers, it is much more likely that FV will exceed the carrying amount but in an exceptional circumstance where the FV is lower, the group depreciation charge would be lower.)

Groups – impairment and NCI

Suggested mark allocation in an FR question (CR Q2): 5 marks

If the NCI is based on the **fair value** or "full goodwill" method, there is no complication here

> Allocate an impairment loss against both the parent's goodwill and the NCI figure

If the NCI is based on the **proportion of net assets** method, it is necessary to apply a "**notional goodwill**" approach as explained in this section

This is because under the proportion of net assets the NCI is valued purely on the basis of net assets whereas goodwill is, by definition, a **difference** over and above consideration paid as compared to net assets i.e. it is an **additional** amount over and above net assets

Notional goodwill adjustment – calculation of the figure

Leave the parent's calculated goodwill figure as it is – no adjustment here

The notional NCI goodwill is calculated by **grossing up** the above parent figure and taking the NCI share of this

For example, if the NCI is 20% then apply a fraction of 20/80 or if the NCI is 30% then apply a fraction of 30/70, and so on

The result of this calculation will then "**absorb**" some of the total impairment loss, rather than this being taken by the parent – see below

Notional goodwill adjustment – allocation of the impairment loss

After calculating the above notional goodwill figure for the NCI, add it to the NCI value and then allocate the impairment loss based on the parent's goodwill figures and the adjusted (increased) NCI figure

However, the portion allocated to the NCI is only **notional** so it is **not recognised** in the consolidated P&L (only the parent's share is) – make sure you clearly explain this and provide relevant figures

See also **page 117** of these Exam Room Notes

Groups – step acquisition

Suggested mark allocation in an FR question (CR Q2): 6 marks

Here the parent acquires control over the subsidiary in **stages**, by buying **blocks** of shares at different times

Full IFRS 3 acquisition accounting should only be applied when **control** has been achieved – until control is achieved any pre-existing interest is accounted for in accordance with IFRS 9 for **investments** and IAS 28 for **associates and joint ventures**

If the 50% boundary is crossed, the entity should **revalue** its holding and report any **gain or loss** in profit or loss for the year – if the 50% boundary is not crossed, no gain or loss is reported and instead there is an adjustment to the parent's **equity**

There are 3 potential scenarios

> **Investment** to subsidiary (e.g. 10% holding to 60% holding)
>
> **Associate** to subsidiary (e.g. 35% holding to 60% holding)
>
> Increase in a holding which was **already** a controlling holding (e.g. 55% to 60% holding)

Scenarios 1 and 2 – Investment or Associate becomes a subsidiary

Consideration paid to acquire control (at fair value)	X
NCI (either at fair value or the proportion of net assets method)	X
Fair value of previously held equity interest at acquisition date	X
Less fair value of net assets of acquiree	(X)
= Goodwill	

In other words, compare what you are **now paying** and the value of what you **currently hold** against the value of all the net assets of the acquired entity, net of the NCI.

Reclassification adjustments on achieving control

If the previously held equity was classified as an **investment in an equity accounted associate** and a share in the associate's **revaluation surplus** was recognised, this surplus should now be **transferred within reserves** from the **revaluation surplus** to **retained earnings**

Scenario 3 – Acquisitions that do not result in a change of control

No gain or loss is recognised

Goodwill is not re-measured

© ACA Simplified 2019. No copying or reproduction permitted.

Groups – step acquisition

The difference between the fair value of consideration paid and the change in the NCI is recognised directly in **equity attributable** to owners of the parent

For example, if the entity **already** has **control** of a subsidiary and purchases a **further 10%** shareholding for £200,000 resulting in the NCI decreasing by £150,000 (as the NCI no longer holds the 10% sold) then a balancing amount of £50,000 would be debited from the parent's equity

Debit	NCI	150,000
Debit	Shareholders' equity	50,000 (balancing figure)
Credit	Cash	200,000

(Note – the balancing figure could be a Credit entry depending on the relationship between the value of the consideration paid and the size of the reduction in the NCI: our Debit entry in the example above is simply for illustrative purposes.)

Groups – step disposal

Suggested mark allocation in an FR question (CR Q2): 6 marks

There are 3 potential scenarios

- Subsidiary to **Associate** (e.g. 70% holding to 30% holding)
- Subsidiary to **Investment** (e.g. 70% holding to 15% holding)
- Subsidiary to **subsidiary** (e.g. 70% holding to 60% holding)

As in the case of step acquisitions, the first 2 scenarios can apply the same pro forma approach

Remember that there may be a link to **IFRS 5** in relation to discontinued operations as a result of the disposal – see **page 27** of this book for relevant notes – if the discontinued operations rules do not apply, the results of the previous subsidiary company must be **consolidated** into the group accounts as **continued** operations through to the date of sale

Scenarios 1 and 2 – subsidiary to Associate and subsidiary to Investment

Here there is a loss of control so a gain or loss on disposal is calculated using the following formula

Proceeds	X
Fair value of interest retained	X
less net assets of subsidiary prior to disposal (Working)	(X)
= Profit/Loss	X/(X)

Working	
Net assets	X
Goodwill at disposal	X
less NCI	(X)
= net assets of subsidiary prior to disposal	X

For a subsidiary to Associate disposal

Equity account as normal by reference to the year-end holding – the carrying value of the associate is based on the fair value of the interest as included within the gain calculation pro forma above

Consolidate results up to the date of disposal based on the pre-disposal holding

Equity account for results after the date of disposal based on the post disposal holding

Include the gain or loss on disposal as calculated in the pro forma

Groups – step disposal

Amounts recognised in OCI in relation to the subsidiary should be accounted for in the same way as if the parent company had directly disposed of the relevant assets i.e. transfer a revaluation surplus into group retained earnings for revalued assets

For a subsidiary to Investment disposal

The interest retained is initially recorded at the fair value which was included within the gain calculation pro forma above

Consolidate results up to the date of disposal based on the pre-disposal holding

Include dividend income after the date of disposal

Include the gain or loss on disposal as calculated above

Amounts recognised in OCI in relation to the subsidiary should be accounted for in the same way as if the parent company had directly disposed of the relevant assets i.e. transfer a revaluation surplus into group retained earnings for revalued assets

Subsidiary to associate or investment – not just a matter of the shareholding %

Note that you may need to consider more than the remaining shareholding percentage to determine whether an entity now holds an associate, or just a simple investment

"Significant influence" is defined as the "power to participate" but not to control – if the entity has "significant influence" then associate status applies

"Significant influence" is presumed to exist if an investor holds 20% or more of the voting power of the investee unless it can be shown that this is clearly not the case

If the entity holds less than 20% it may nevertheless still have "significant influence" based on other factors such as:

> if the entity can control the board of directors with majority decisions

> if there are material transactions between the 2 companies such as the previous parent company providing important products or services to the previous subsidiary company

If the holding is an associate then IAS 28 requires the use of the equity method to account for investments in associates

Remember that there may be a link to IFRS 5 in relation to discontinued operations as a result of the disposal – see **page 27** of this book for relevant notes – if the discontinued operations rules do not apply, the results of the previous subsidiary company must be **consolidated** into the group accounts as **continued** operations through to the date of sale

Are the operations discontinued?

To be presented as discontinued, the sale of shares in a subsidiary needs to be part of a single coordinated plan to withdraw from a major business line

If there are continuing commercial links between the previous parent company and previous subsidiary company then there may not necessarily be a discontinued operation and the results of the previous

Groups – step disposal

subsidiary company should be consolidated into the group accounts as continuing operations through to the date of sale

Scenario 3 – subsidiary to subsidiary

Here there is no loss of control – therefore no gain or loss on disposal is calculated and no adjustment is made to the carrying value of goodwill. The difference between the proceeds received and the increase in the NCI (since entities other than the parent now have an increased shareholding) is accounted for in shareholder's equity i.e. as a balancing entry to shareholder's equity:

Debit	Proceeds (Cash or Receivables)	70,000
Credit	NCI	30,000
Credit	Shareholders' equity	40,000 (balancing figure)

(Note – the balancing figure could be a Debit entry depending on the relationship between the value of the proceeds and the size of the increase in NCI: our Credit entry in the example above is simply for illustrative purposes.)

Part disposal from an Associate holding (Associate to Investment)

For example, there may be a change from 40% holding to a 10% holding

Here there is a loss of significant influence so a gain or loss on disposal is calculated using the following formula

Proceeds	X
Fair value of interest retained	X
less Working (see below)	(X)
Profit/Loss	X/(X)

Working	
Cost of investment	X
Share of post-acquisition profits retained by Associate at disposal	X
Impairment of investment to date	(X)

The interest retained is initially recorded at **fair value**, as included within the gain calculation

Equity account for results up to the date of disposal based on the pre-disposal holding

Include dividends received after the date of disposal as dividend income

Include gain or loss on disposal as calculated above

Groups – subsidiary

Suggested mark allocation in an FR question (CR Q2): 6-8 marks for consideration of control and the goodwill calculation

Treatment

Is "control" achieved?

Under IFRS 10, an acquisition should be treated as a subsidiary and therefore consolidated if ownership indicates "control" of the entity

Ownership of more than 50% of share capital is a strong indicator that the owner has more than half of the voting power and therefore has "control"

Assessing control under IFRS 10 – advanced points

Note – only include these points if the matter of control appears complicated in the scenario – in most group answers, you would not need the below details

IFRS 10 states that an investor controls an investee if and only if it has all the following

   power over the investee

   exposure, or rights, to variable returns from its involvement with the investee

   the ability to use its power over the investee to affect the amount of the investor's returns

The fact that board members may not have actually exercised control in practice is not a determining factor in deciding whether the entity has control over the investee

We also need to consider powers to appoint board members – if there are such appointment powers for board members other than the entity which has a majority shareholding, then the matter may not be so straightforward and the shareholding greater than 50% may not be sufficient to create "control"

In some cases, control of board decisions over a fundamental aspect of the company such as R&D or Finance e.g. if the owner can appoint a specific Director to be the head of R&D or Finance could also confer control if that division is fundamental to the investee

The right to acquire further shares through a call option could also be relevant – IFRS 10 requires an investor to consider potential voting rights in considering whether it has control and whether the right is substantive i.e. whether the holder has the practical ability to exercise the right

If "control" is not held, the investment cannot be recognised as a subsidiary and would be recognised instead as an associate

Goodwill calculation

See **page 89** of these Exam Room Notes.

Remember that **IFRS 3** requires all assets and liabilities to be stated at **fair value** – look out for additional asset value and contingent liabilities which will affect the net assets position

Contingent liabilities are not **recognised** in the individual statements but per IFRS 3 such liabilities must be **recognised** at **fair value** in the goodwill calculation

Groups – subsidiary to associate

Suggested mark allocation in an FR question (CR Q2): 4 marks

Remember to **time apportion** the treatment – treat as a **subsidiary** for the months during the year until disposal takes place – this would mean **consolidating** in the relevant number of months to the CSPL and recording an NCI at the relevant percentage at the end of the same period

After disposal, check whether there is still an **ability to influence** the disposed of subsidiary e.g. the ability to appoint directors to the board

If so, state that the entity should be treated as an **associate** and the **equity accounting method** should be used for the remaining X months of the year (the months **following** the sale)

> State that in future years the entity will make a **lower contribution to group profit** due to the **reduction** in the **percentage** investment held

State that a gain or loss on disposal occurs and calculate this if possible – use the following pro forma

Proceeds	X
FV of interest retained	X
NCI at disposal	X
less net assets at disposal	(X)
less remaining goodwill at disposal	(X)
Gain or loss on disposal	X

Check for any **dividends** – if these are declared whilst the entity is **still a subsidiary** then they should be **eliminated** on consolidation but if the dividend is physically paid **after** the disposal (and thus after the change to an associate) then remember **not to deduct** the amount from the net assets at disposal (as the **cash** is still held)

Groups – subsidiary to subsidiary

Suggested mark allocation in an FR question (CR Q2): 4 marks

Example: an entity holds 80% of a subsidiary and sells 20% of the subsidiary

Treatment

The subsidiary **remains** a subsidiary – under IFRS 3 there is **no disposal** but rather a transaction between group shareholders – there is no crossing of an accounting boundary which will result in any change in control so **no gain or loss** will be recorded – a **fair value** exercise is **not** required

The parent is treated as **selling a stake** (e.g. 20%) **to the NCI**

The NCI is **increased** in the SFP to reflect its greater share of the subsidiary

The difference between the consideration received from the NCI and the increase in the NCI (i.e. the value of the additional share now owned by the NCI) is taken as an adjustment to the parent's equity by crediting or debiting the group retained earnings

Consideration received	X
Increase in NCI on disposal	(X)
Adjustment to parent's equity (through group retained earnings)	X

The matter does not affect the **trading** profit of the company and so has no impact on the **P&L** or **EPS**

Hedge accounting – cash flow hedge

Suggested mark allocation in an FR question (CR Q2): 4 marks

Note – as IFRS 9 is now the primary examinable standard in relation to hedge accounting, the notes in this section are based on IFRS 9. However, entities retain the right to apply the previous IAS 39 hedge accounting rules if they wish so (in line with the Advanced Level Study Manuals which continue to provide notes and explanations in relation to IAS 39 hedge accounting rules) we have provided a summary comparison between IFRS 9 and IAS 39 rules in our **Hedge accounting – IFRS 9 versus IAS 39** section starting on **page 113** of this set of *Exam Room Notes*.

General process

State why the hedge is being treated as a **cash flow** hedge – the entity is hedging a **variability** in cash flows for currency or other reasons (e.g. interest rate changes on a loan)

> A **firm commitment** is a binding agreement for the exchange of a **specified quantity** of resources at a specified price on a specified future date or dates – a **foreign currency** firm commitment can be subject to **either** a **cash flow** hedge or a **fair value** hedge
>
> **Tip** – a firm **commitment** involving a **foreign currency** transaction is therefore a difficult kind of scenario because it can be **either** a cash flow hedge **or** a fair value hedge – you may be able to remember this by thinking that (just as in other areas of life!) "**commitment is difficult**"
>
> A **firm commitment** (the item being hedged) is not **recognised** – however the existence of the contract and associated risk would be **disclosed** from the inception date in accordance with IFRS 7
>
> A **firm commitment account** may be needed to recognise an asset or liability (depending on exchange rate movement) as the opposite side of the derivative transaction
>
> A hedge of a **forecast transaction** (an uncommitted but anticipated future transaction) **must** be a **cash flow hedge** – the forecast transaction should be **specifically identifiable** (i.e. not something such as "the last 5,000 units produced"), **highly probable** and with a **party external** to the entity – the documentation should identify the **date** on which, or time period in which, the forecast transaction is **expected to occur** (the exact date is not required, but a reasonably specific and narrow range of dates should be stated)

Recognise entries at **inception** of the hedge – note that **often** the **derivative** will have **zero fair value** on this day and there may be no related cash transaction to record so there will be no figure to recognise for the derivative at inception – however, if the derivative is an option, for example, then **cash** may have been spent on the **premium** and this **cost should be capitalised** into the asset as an initially recognised amount

Even if no amounts are recognised at inception, the existence of the contract and associated risk should be **disclosed** from the **inception** date in accordance with IFRS 7

Any **transaction costs** such as professional fees should be **expensed**

Update entries at the year-end – the derivative will have gained or lost fair value with an **opposite** entry to the **P&L** for the underlying the hedged item

> Perform an effectiveness test by applying the 3 effectiveness criteria within IFRS 9:

Hedge accounting – cash flow hedge

(1) there is an economic relationship between the hedged item and the hedging instrument i.e. the hedging instrument and the hedged item have values that generally move in the opposite direction because of the same risk, which is the hedged risk

(2) the effect of credit risk does not dominate the value changes that result from that economic relationship i.e. the value changes due to credit risk are not a significant driver of the value changes of either the hedging instrument or the hedged item

(3) the hedge ratio of the hedging relationship (quantity of hedging instrument vs quantity of hedged item) is the same as that resulting from the quantity of the hedged item that the entity actually hedges and the quantity of the hedging instrument that the entity actually uses to hedge that quantity of hedged item

For a **cash flow hedge**, the effective portion (i.e. the movement in the derivative **up to** the movement in the hedged item) is **recorded in OCI and held in a cash flow reserve** until the transaction takes place – any other portion ("ineffective") is put through the P&L (except in the case of the OCI option for equity investments)

The amount stored is **released** into the P&L over the same period that the underlying item has its effect on the P&L e.g. as depreciation or interest expense/income hits the P&L

Treatment at inception and at year end

Recognise the cost of the derivative itself on the SFP (but **expense** any transaction costs such as professional fees)

    Dr Derivative asset

    Cr Cash/Payables

Review the hedge for **effectiveness** under the 3 effectiveness criteria within IFRS 9 (see above)

Update the derivative asset/liability for the **fair value at the end of the year** – the **effective** portion is taken through **OCI** and the **ineffective** portion must be recognised in the **P&L**

Recycle any amounts of stored up in OCI into the P&L over the same period that the **underlying item affects the P&L**

Treatment – fixed price option

If the hedged contract is a fixed price option (i.e. an option to purchase a machine for $5m with no specification of an exchange rate to apply) then the fair value at inception is $5m translated into sterling at the spot rate – this is because we can determine what it would be reasonable to pay in sterling for the right to buy the machine at $5m

This will give the derivative an initial fair value at **inception** – the fair value at the **reporting date** will then be $5m divided by the closing rate

Please note that this is a different treatment to a **currency option** which will normally have a **nil** value at inception as exchange rates will not have moved on the inception day so there is no FV to recognise

Hedge accounting – cash flow hedge

Possible purchase of a machine

If the question wording refers to a "**highly probable**" transaction then this is a reference to an "forecast transaction" and **must** therefore imply that you need to look at a **cash flow** hedge (since a fair value hedge can only be applied to an "firm commitment" – fair value hedging cannot be applied to a "forecast transaction")

Remember **not** to **recognise** the machine in the financial statements until the **risks and rewards** of **ownership** have been transferred to the entity (this does not happen simply because a transaction is highly probable i.e. just because hedge accounting can be applied does not mean that the underlying item is recognised in the financial statements) – it is quite common for an exam question to try to trick you into prematurely **capitalising** equipment simply because there is a highly probable forecast transaction (the client accountant may already have made this mistake)

Summary of conditions for hedge accounting

At inception of the hedge, there is a **formal designation and documentation** of the hedging relationship and the entity's **risk management objective** and **strategy** for undertaking the hedge

The hedging relationship meets all 3 of the IFRS 9 effectiveness criteria

The hedge is **assessed for effectiveness** on an **ongoing basis**

In respect of a **cash flow hedge**, a forecast transaction is **highly probable**

Hedge accounting – fair value hedge

Suggested mark allocation in an FR question (CR Q2): 4 marks

Note – as IFRS 9 is now the primary examinable standard in relation to hedge accounting, the notes in this section are based on IFRS 9. However, entities retain the right to apply the previous IAS 39 hedge accounting rules if they wish so (in line with the Advanced Level Study Manuals which continue to provide notes and explanations in relation to IAS 39 hedge accounting rules) we have provided a summary comparison between IFRS 9 and IAS 39 rules in our **Hedge accounting – IFRS 9 versus IAS 39** section starting on **page 113** of this set of *Exam Room Notes*.

General process

State **why** the hedge is being treated as a **fair value** hedge – the entity is concerned that the underlying item could have a less favourable fair value at the time the transaction takes place

A **firm commitment** (the item being hedged) is not **recognised** – however the existence of the contract and associated risk would be **disclosed** from the inception date in accordance with IFRS 7

Recognise entries at **inception** of the hedge – note that **often** the **derivative** will have **zero fair value** on this day and there may be no related cash transaction to record so there will be no figure to recognise for the derivative at inception – however, if the derivative is an option, for example, then **cash** may have been spent on the **premium** and this **cost should be capitalised** into the asset as an initially recognised amount

Even if no amounts are recognised at inception, the existence of the contract and associated risk should be **disclosed** from the **inception** date in accordance with IFRS 7

Any **transaction costs** such as professional fees should be **expensed**

Update entries at the year-end – the derivative will have gained or lost fair value with an **opposite** entry to the **P&L** for the underlying hedged item

> Perform an assessment under the 3 effectiveness criteria within IFRS 9:
>
> (1) there is an economic relationship between the hedged item and the hedging instrument i.e. the hedging instrument and the hedged item have values that generally move in the opposite direction because of the same risk, which is the hedged risk
>
> (2) the effect of credit risk does not dominate the value changes that result from that economic relationship i.e. the value changes due to credit risk are not a significant driver of the value changes of either the hedging instrument or the hedged item
>
> (3) the hedge ratio of the hedging relationship (quantity of hedging instrument vs quantity of hedged item) is the same as that resulting from the quantity of the hedged item that the entity actually hedges and the quantity of the hedging instrument that the entity actually uses to hedge that quantity of hedged item

A **firm commitment account** may be needed to recognise an asset or liability (depending on exchange rate movement) as the opposite side of the derivative transaction

For a fair value hedge, the accounting is relatively straightforward as **both** movements in the value of the hedged item and hedging instruments go into the P&L (except in the case of the OCI option for equity investments)

Hedge accounting – fair value hedge

Foreign currency firm commitment

A hedge of a **foreign currency firm commitment** may be accounted for as a FV hedge **or** as a cash flow hedge at the **choice of the entity**

> **Tip** – a firm **commitment** involving a **foreign currency** transaction is therefore a difficult kind of scenario because it can be **either** a cash flow hedge **or** a fair value hedge – you may be able to remember this by thinking that (just as in other areas of life!) "**commitment is difficult**"
>
> A firm commitment is a **binding agreement** for the exchange of a specified quantity of resources at a specified price on a specified future date or dates
>
> A hedge of a **forecast** transaction (an uncommitted but anticipated future transaction) must be a cash flow hedge

If the hedged risk is identified as the forward exchange rate, rather than the spot rate, then it could be assumed to be perfectly effective if a forward is taken out as the hedging instrument

Final entries in a FV hedge – example of hedge of a purchase of inventories

On settlement, the inventory is purchased at the agreed rate, translated at the spot rate on the day of purchase

The value of the **firm commitment** then needs to be removed from the SFP, **adjusting the initial carrying amount of the inventory** as the other side of the double entry – this should set the effective purchase price (spot rate on the date of purchase, adjusted for hedging gain or loss) to that involved in the **initial** exchange rate when the hedge was set up

For example, if the **FV of the inventory has increased** since the hedge was set up, a firm commitment **liability** will have built up over time – this is then debited to close the account down at settlement and the credit side goes against inventory to reduce the cost of that purchase down to what it would have been at the time the hedge was set up (i.e. fixing it to that initial amount)

When using **FV hedging**, do not forget to **adjust** the **initial carrying amount** of the hedged item for this aspect to ensure that the entity has not gained nor lost out as a result of changes over time

Summary of conditions for hedge accounting

At inception of the hedge, there is a **formal designation and documentation** of the hedging relationship and the entity's **risk management objective** and **strategy** for undertaking the hedge

The hedging relationship meets all 3 of the IFRS 9 effectiveness criteria

The hedge is **assessed for effectiveness** on an **ongoing basis**

Hedge accounting – general

Note – as IFRS 9 is now the primary examinable standard in relation to hedge accounting, the notes in this section are based on IFRS 9. However, entities retain the right to apply the previous IAS 39 hedge accounting rules if they wish so (in line with the Advanced Level Study Manuals which continue to provide notes and explanations in relation to IAS 39 hedge accounting rules) we have provided a summary comparison between IFRS 9 and IAS 39 rules in our **Hedge accounting – IFRS 9 versus IAS 39** section starting on **page 113** of this set of *Exam Room Notes*.

The reason to apply hedge accounting is to ensure that the changes in value in the hedged item and changes in value in the hedging instrument are reflected in the financial statements in the **same period**

Derivatives are always measured at **FVtPL** but the underlying hedged item **may not be** – applying hedge accounting creates an accounting alignment

IFRS 9 requires the hedge to be **designated** and **documented** at inception – documentation cannot be **backdated** and hedge accounting cannot be applied **retrospectively**

The **effectiveness** of the hedge must be tested **at least every reporting date**

Hedge documentation – points which should be included

Formal designation and documentation of the hedging relationship and the entity's risk management objective and strategy for undertaking the hedge

Identification of the hedged item, the hedging instrument, the nature of the hedged risk and how the entity will assess whether the hedging relationship meets the hedge effectiveness requirements (including its analysis of the sources of hedge ineffectiveness and how it determines the hedge ratio)

Derivative instruments

Transaction cost versus instrument cost

Be careful – **transaction costs** such as professional fees should **not** be treated as resulting in an **initial cost** for the item but if the item has a **cost to purchase** (e.g. the premium on an option) then this amount **should** be treated as part of the **initial cost** of the item and **capitalised** – therefore changes in fair value at the year-end should take into account this initial cost (i.e. deduct the cost from the year-end FV to find the movement to take to the P&L)

Therefore if the question only mentions **transaction costs** then the item will have a **nil value** at inception – if the question mentions **other types of cost** then the item will **not** have a **nil value** at inception

Example – a purchased option costs £50,000 and has a fair value of £1m at the year-end – the initial cost recognised is £50,000 and the movement in fair value is £950,000 for the year (not £1m)

Hedge accounting – hedge of a net investment

Suggested mark allocation in an FR question (CR Q2): 4 marks

Note – as IFRS 9 is now the primary examinable standard in relation to hedge accounting, the notes in this section are based on IFRS 9. However, entities retain the right to apply the previous IAS 39 hedge accounting rules if they wish so (in line with the Advanced Level Study Manuals which continue to provide notes and explanations in relation to IAS 39 hedge accounting rules) we have provided a summary comparison between IFRS 9 and IAS 39 rules in our **Hedge accounting – IFRS 9 versus IAS 39** section starting on **page 113** of this set of *Exam Room Notes*.

This type of hedge only applies to a **group** scenario – the parent company takes out a **liability** in a foreign currency to create an opposite movement which hedges its **asset** i.e. a subsidiary which uses that same foreign currency

If the subsidiary **loses** value due to a change in the exchange rate, the company will experience a **counterbalancing gain** on its liability, and vice versa

This type of hedge is treated like a **cash flow hedge** i.e. the **ineffective** portion should be recognised in the **P&L** with the **effective** portion being recognised in **OCI**

Hedge documentation

The usual hedge documentation is required for this hedge i.e.

> Formal designation and documentation of the hedging relationship and the entity's risk management objective and strategy for undertaking the hedge

> Identification of the hedged item, the hedging instrument, the nature of the hedged risk and how the entity will assess whether the hedging relationship meets the hedge effectiveness requirements (including its analysis of the sources of hedge ineffectiveness and how it determines the hedge ratio)

Treatment

The usual 3 effectiveness criteria within IFRS 9 must be met in the case of this type of hedge:

> (1) there is an economic relationship between the hedged item and the hedging instrument i.e. the hedging instrument and the hedged item have values that generally move in the opposite direction because of the same risk, which is the hedged risk

> (2) the effect of credit risk does not dominate the value changes that result from that economic relationship i.e. the value changes due to credit risk are not a significant driver of the value changes of either the hedging instrument or the hedged item

> (3) the hedge ratio of the hedging relationship (quantity of hedging instrument vs quantity of hedged item) is the same as that resulting from the quantity of the hedged item that the entity actually hedges and the quantity of the hedging instrument that the entity actually uses to hedge that quantity of hedged item

Hedge accounting – hedge of a net investment

You should compare the **loss/gain** on translation of the net investment with the exchange **loss/gain** on the hedging loan

The portion of the gain/loss on the loan which relates to the parent's translation gain/loss in the **translation reserve** should be recognised in OCI and therefore directly in equity – the balance affects the **NCI**

The **ineffective** portion should be recognised in the **P&L** for the year – therefore if the loan moves by **more** than the change in the parent's translation reserve then the **excess amount** goes to the P&L and **not** through **OCI**

Hedge accounting – IFRS 9 detailed rules

Problems with IAS 39 hedge accounting rules

Considered to be **complex** and not reflective of the way in which an entity normally **manages** its risks

Often **prevents entities applying hedge accounting** to transactions which have **genuinely** been entered into for hedging purposes and which do involve a hedging effect **in practice**

IFRS 9 – impact on the entity and auditors

IFRS 9 is effective for reporting periods commencing on or after **1 January 2018**

Adoption of IFRS 9 rules on hedge accounting will require the **entity** to have appropriate processes in place to identify **new hedging opportunities** and to ensure that the extensive new disclosure requirements of IFRS 9 are met

Auditors will need to test management's judgements with regard to the hedge effectiveness criteria (the "**economic relationship**" test – see below) and will also need to obtain comfort over the fair value measurement of the components of non-financial hedged items, purchased options, forward contracts and cross currency swaps

IFRS 9 approach – basics

Applies a **principles-based** approach (compared to the **rules-based** approach of IAS 39)

Use of a principles-based approach will require **judgement** in relation to the determination of whether a hedging relationship meets the **hedge effectiveness criteria** (the "economic relationship" test – see below) and the determination of when "**rebalancing**" will be required (see below)

Aims at **better alignment** with the risk management practices actually used by **management**, allowing transactions which are **genuinely intended to be hedges** to **apply hedge accounting** in situations where **IAS 39 rules may preclude this**

Allows **both** derivatives and non-derivative financial assets or liabilities to be hedging instruments, provided that they are measured at Fair Value through Profit or Loss – IAS 39 requires hedging instruments to be **derivatives** except for the hedge of foreign currency

Replaces the **IAS 39 "bright line" 80% - 125% test** with an "**objective-based assessment**", designed to create an assessment more closely aligned with the actual practices of companies in managing their risks

Requires an "**economic relationship**" between the hedged item and hedging instrument – in other words, the hedging instrument and the hedged item must have values that generally move in opposite directions because of the same risk (which is the hedged risk)

Allows **changes to the hedging relationship** if the risk management objective for that designated hedging relationship remains the same – this is known as "**rebalancing**" – IAS 39 generally requires discontinuation of hedge accounting if there is a change in the hedging relationship

Hedge accounting – IFRS 9 detailed rules

Arrangements at inception

In order to apply the special hedge accounting rules, IFRS 9 requires the hedge to be designated and documented at inception, and the effectiveness of the hedge to be tested at least every reporting date

If the hedge was not formally designated and documented at inception, the entity will not be permitted to apply hedge accounting

IFRS 9 does not permit documentation to be backdated nor for hedge accounting to be applied retrospectively

For audit purposes and to meet the requirements of IFRS 9, the entity would normally be expected to have the following documentation available:

- details of the risk management objectives and the strategy for undertaking the hedge
- identification and description of the hedging instrument
- details of the hedged item or transactions
- nature of the risk being hedged
- description of how the entity will assess the hedging instrument's effectiveness

Hedging criteria

IFRS 9 applies an objective-based test that focuses on the economic relationship between the hedged item and the hedging instrument and the effect of credit risk on that economic relationship

IFRS 9 allows treatment as either a fair value or cash flow hedge

IFRS 9 has an objective-based assessment for hedge effectiveness, under which the following criteria must be met

(1) there is an economic relationship between the hedged item and the hedging instrument i.e. the hedging instrument and the hedged item have values that generally move in the opposite direction because of the same risk, which is the hedged risk

(2) the effect of credit risk does not dominate the value changes that result from that economic relationship i.e. the value changes due to credit risk are not a significant driver of the value changes of either the hedging instrument or the hedged item

(3) the hedge ratio of the hedging relationship (quantity of hedging instrument vs quantity of hedged item) is the same as that resulting from the quantity of the hedged item that the entity actually hedges and the quantity of the hedging instrument that the entity actually uses to hedge that quantity of hedged item

IFRS 9 approach – discontinuation of hedge accounting

Voluntary discontinuation of hedge accounting is **not permitted** when the risk management objective for the hedging relationship has not changed

This is a notable **contrast** with IAS 39 rules which allow an entity to **revoke hedge accounting at any time**

Hedge accounting – IFRS 9 detailed rules

As such, **discontinuation** of hedge accounting is a **rare instance** where the **IFRS 9** rules are **less flexible** than the **IAS 39** rules

IFRS 9 and IAS 39 – shared rules

The following 4 points have not changed under the IFRS 9 approach

the **terminology** of the standards is generally the same

the **3 types** of hedge (fair value hedge, cash flow hedge and hedge of a net investment) are the same

hedge **ineffectiveness** is recognised in **profit or loss** (except for the Other Comprehensive Income option for equity investments, which is a category only available under IFRS 9)

hedge accounting with **written options is prohibited**

IFRS 9 approach – more complex points

Allows the **time value** of purchased options and the **forward element** of forward contracts and foreign currency basis spreads to be **excluded** from the hedging relationship, which should decrease volatility in profit or loss – under IFRS 9 the time component of an option is a cost of hedging presented through **OCI** (rather than in the P&L) and the forward element of forward contracts may also be presented in **OCI** (rather than in the P&L)

Allows **more items** to be designated as **hedged items** than under IAS 39 – examples include risk components of non-financial items, groups of items and net positions even if the change in value attributable to the hedged risk is not proportional to that of the designated items within the group (unlike under IAS 39), and equity investments at Fair Value through Other Comprehensive Income (this category does not exist under IAS 39)

May be beneficial to **banks** – under IAS 39, banks do not often achieve hedge accounting on the **credit risk of exposures** due to certain complications with the rules – IFRS 9 will make it easier to achieve hedge accounting on this type of risk

Does **not permit** hedge accounting to apply when **credit risk dominates the value changes** that result from an otherwise qualifying "economic relationship"

Hedging of an equity investment at FVtOCI

IFRS 9 states that if the hedging instrument hedges an equity investment at fair value through OCI, the gain or loss on the hedging instrument is recognised in OCI

Since hedge accounting is applied, any loss on revaluing the investment should be charged to OCI in accordance with the IFRS 9 treatment of fair value hedges – it is therefore possible that no adjusting entries would be required because the loss would be recorded in OCI irrespective of the hedge accounting rules

Intrinsic value of options over shares and hedge accounting

IFRS 9 hedge accounting rules require a loss on shares to be matched in OCI against the gain on the intrinsic element of options (the hedging instrument) so an increase in the intrinsic value of options would be recorded in OCI rather than in the P&L (as would be usual)

Receivables do not require hedge accounting

An exchange difference on a receivable and related derivative would both be recognised through profit or loss so there would be no need to apply the hedge accounting provisions

A receivable is a financial instrument and is therefore subject to IFRS 9 and scoped out of IAS 37

Hedge accounting – IFRS 9 versus IAS 39

	IAS 39	IFRS 9
Eligibility of hedging instruments	Derivatives may be designated as hedging instruments Nonderivatives may be designated as hedging instruments only for hedges of foreign currency risk	Any financial instrument may be a hedging instrument if it is measured at fair value through profit or loss

Therefore, under IAS 39, non-derivative items are less widely used as hedging instruments than under IFRS 9

	IAS 39	IFRS 9
Eligibility of hedged items	Recognised assets, liabilities, firm commitments, highly probable forecast transactions and net investments in foreign operations may be designated as hedged items In some circumstances, risk components of the financial asset or liability may be designated as a hedged item	In addition to IAS 39 eligible hedged items, IFRS 9 allows a risk component of a non-financial asset or liability to be designated as a hedged item in some circumstances

Therefore, fewer items can be designated as hedged items under IAS 39

	IAS 39	IFRS 9
Qualifying criteria for applying hedge accounting	A hedging relationship only qualifies for hedge accounting if certain criteria are met, including a quantitative hedge effectiveness test under which hedge effectiveness must fall in the range 80% to 125%	Hedge effectiveness criteria are principles-based and aligned with risk management activities

Therefore, genuine hedging relationships captured by IFRS 9 may be missed when applying IAS 39 rules

Hedge accounting – IFRS 9 versus IAS 39

	IAS 39	IFRS 9
Rebalancing	The concept of rebalancing does not exist within IAS 39	Rebalancing is permitted by IFRS 9 in some circumstances

Lack of guidance on rebalancing means that hedge accounting needs to be discontinued under IAS 39 while it could continue under IFRS 9

	IAS 39	IFRS 9
Discontinuation of hedging relationships	Hedge accounting may be discontinued at any time	Hedge accounting may not be discontinued where the hedging relationship continues to meet qualifying criteria – can only discontinue when qualifying criteria are no longer met

	IAS 39	IFRS 9
Accounting for the time value component of options and forward contracts	The part of an option that reflects time value and the forward element of a forward contract are treated as derivatives held for trading purposes	The time value component of an option is a cost of hedging presented in OCI The forward element of a forward contract may also be presented in OCI

Therefore, IAS 39 leads to greater volatility in profit or loss than IFRS 9

Holiday pay accrual

Suggested mark allocation in an FR question (CR Q2): 2 marks

Treatment

IAS 19 requires an accrual to be made for **holiday entitlement carried forward** to the next year

Calculate (1) the number of days carried forward **on average per employee**

Calculate (2) entity's **total number of working days in a year** e.g. number of employees multiplied by (purely as an example) 48 weeks x 5 days per week or 240 days (check the question wording to determine the number of working days in the year for the entity)

The accrual should then be based on the **(1) number of days carried forward** divided by **(2) the total number of working days in the entity's working year** multiplied by **total annual salary costs**

In other words you are finding the share of total annual salary costs which relates to the proportion of days carried forward to the next year as holiday

The journal is likely to be

        Dr   Employee expenses (P&L)

        Cr   Accruals (SFP)

Impairment

Suggested mark allocation in an FR question (CR Q2): 4-8 marks

Assets should not be carried at more than their **recoverable amount** which is the **higher** of **value in use** and **FV less CTS**

>Value in use is the **present value** of the **future cash flows** expected to be derived from an asset (**excluding** finance and tax costs)

Impairment is recognised **immediately** in profit or loss unless the asset has **previously been revalued**, in which case it is treated as a **revaluation decrease** and not as an impairment loss (it is first set against the revaluation surplus on the same asset, with any excess being recognised in profit or loss)

Indicators of impairment

Only **material** impairment needs to be identified – if there are indicators of **possible** impairment, the entity is required to make a formal estimate of the recoverable amount of the assets concerned

External indicators

A **fall** in the asset's market value that is more significant than would **normally** be **expected** from the passage of time through normal use

A significant **change** in the technological, market, legal or economic **environment** of the business in which the assets are employed

An **increase** in market interest rates or market rates of return on investments likely to affect the **discount rate** used in calculating **value in use**

Carrying amount of the entity's net assets being more than its **market capitalisation**

Internal indicators

Evidence of **obsolescence** or **physical damage**

Adverse changes in the **use** to which the asset is put

Indications that the **economic performance** of an asset is, or will be, **worse than expected**

Always perform annual impairment tests on the following 2 items

>An intangible asset with an **indefinite** useful life

>**Goodwill** acquired in a business combination

Asset with a revaluation surplus

First recognise the **impairment** against the revaluation surplus

If there is still a further amount to recognise **after the revaluation surplus** has been reduced to **nil** then the **remainder** of the impairment charge should be recognised as part of **profit or loss**

Impairment – CGU

Suggested mark allocation in an FR question (CR Q2): 6 marks

Anticipated **future losses** indicate that equipment/a CGU could be **impaired**

The impairment review involves comparing the **carrying amount** of the equipment in the financial statements with the **recoverable amount** – if the recoverable amount is **lower** than the carrying amount, the difference should be **written off** in the **P&L** for the year and **deducted** from the **carrying amount** in the **SFP**

Recoverable amount is defined as the **higher** of

> FV less CTS
>
> value in use

FV less CTS is the price that would be received in an **orderly** transaction between market participants at the measurement date, net of any selling costs

Value in use is the present value of expected future cash flows from the CGU, discounted at a rate the market would expect for any equally risky investments

Normally the cash flow should be estimated over a **maximum of 5 years** – if a period above this figure is used this should be **disclosed** (the **validity** of the disclosed explanation should be **reviewed** as part of the audit)

Allocation of impairment losses – order of allocation

First allocate as much as possible against **goodwill**

Then allocate against **other assets** on a **pro-rata** basis, based on **carrying value**

> However, **no asset** should be reduced below the **higher** of its **recoverable value** and **zero**
>
>> Therefore assets such as **cash**, **inventories** or **receivables** should **not** take any impairment as these should already be at recoverable value

Treatment of NCI interest in goodwill of a CGU – proportion of net assets method of valuing NCI

Notionally adjust the NCI share in goodwill by grossing it up **temporarily** for impairment purposes only – add this **notional** amount onto the goodwill balance available to be reduced for impairment (i.e. the first target in the allocation of the impairment loss as this is **first allocated** against goodwill and then **pro rata** against other assets)

However, the **actual impairment loss** recognised is the parent's share only – the **notional amount** is only used to determine how the total impairment loss is used up

The consequent impairment loss calculated is only recognised to the extent of the parent's share

Example

An NCI of 40% is valued on the net assets method – goodwill held by the parent is therefore 60% of the total goodwill for notional purposes – therefore NCI share is **40 / 60** x goodwill held by the parent

If the parent's goodwill is 90 then we would add on 40 / 60 x 90 or **60 of notional goodwill** to provide up to **150 of goodwill** against which to allocate impairment but only take the parent's (60%) share of that allocated impairment into account when reducing goodwill and charging the P&L

For example, here we would take only **60%** of the impairment allocated to goodwill when reducing the parent's figure of **90** down to the relevant amount

Under the FV method of valuing NCI no such special adjustment is required before allocating impairment

Reversal of a CGU impairment

Goodwill impairment is not **reversed** once recognised

Impairment of **other assets can** be reversed pro-rata to the carrying amount of those assets

The revised carrying amount may not, however, be increased above the **lower** of

Recoverable amount, and

Depreciated carrying amount assuming that no impairment loss had originally been recognised

The reversal is recognised in the **P&L** except where reversing a loss recognised on assets carried at revalued amounts which are treated in accordance with the applicable IFRS

Insurance Contracts

IFRS 4 was issued in **2004** as an **interim** solution which **permits** the **continued use of pre-existing national reporting frameworks** whilst seeking to prevent **certain undesirable practices** – the standard also aims to **reduce divergence** amongst the practices used in different countries

IFRS 4 specifies the financial reporting for **insurance contracts** by an entity that issues such contracts or holds reinsurance contracts – it only relates to these contracts and **not** to the **assets** and **liabilities** held by insurers **generally**

IFRS 4 focuses largely on improving **disclosure requirements** but contains a number of limited improvements to existing **accounting** requirements – these are **best practice** examples and not requirements if other practices are currently adopted

The contract must relate to an **uncertain event** i.e. an event with **uncertainty** with respect to **at least one** of the following: **occurrence**, **timing** or the **level of compensation** to be paid by the insurer

The contract must have significant **insurance risk** (**non-financial** risk relating to whether an event occurs, rather than a change in a financial variable) or IFRS 4 will not apply

Examples of insurance contracts

Life insurance and prepaid funeral plans

Disability and medical cover

Credit insurance

Travel cover

Examples which are not insurance contracts

Product warranties

Defined benefit pensions

Licences or contractual rights/obligations contingent on the use of a non-financial item

A finance lease with a residual value guarantee

Financial guarantees within the scope of IAS 39 (note: the 2019 edition of the Corporate Reporting Study Manual still refers to IAS 39 (rather than to IFRS 9) in relation to this rule so we have left in place this reference to IAS 39 (rather than to IFRS 9))

Contingent consideration that has arisen as a result of a business combination

Insurance contracts that the entity holds as policyholder

Recognition and measurement

IFRS 4 **exempts** an insurer temporarily from the **usual need to consider the IASB Framework where there is no specific accounting requirement** set out in another international standard – this exemption is **temporary** whilst further rules on insurance contracts are being developed by the IASB

Insurance Contracts

However IFRS 4:

Requires a **liability adequacy test** to be performed

Prohibits **provisions** for possible claims under contracts that are **not in existence** at the reporting date (**catastrophe** or **equalisation** provisions)

Requires an **impairment test** for reinsurance assets – impairment is recognised if an event has occurred that will lead to amounts due under the contract not being recovered in full and a reliable estimate of the shortfall can be assessed

Requires an insurer to continue to **recognise** insurance liabilities until they are discharged, cancelled or expire – offsetting liabilities against related reinsurance assets is not permitted

Liability adequacy test

Recognise insurance liabilities based on the current estimate of future contractual cash flows – recognise any identified shortfall **immediately** as part of the profit or loss for the period i.e. the amount carried in the accounts may not be sufficient compared to this calculated amount

Should be based on **all** contractual cash flows and related costs such as claims handling costs – cash flows relating to embedded options or guarantees should also be included – deduct any deferred acquisition costs and related intangible assets

If the accounting policies of the insurer do not demand a liability adequacy test then the amount that should be recognised under IAS 37 should instead be used, **increasing** the **liability** recognised if necessary

Disclosures

The insurer must disclose

Information which "**identifies and explains amounts arising from insurance contracts**" – accounting policies adopted, identification of recognised assets, liabilities, income and expense arising from insurance contracts

Risk management objectives and policies of an entity should be disclosed to explain how an insurer deals with the **uncertainty** it is exposed to

An entity is not generally required to comply with the disclosure requirements of IFRS 4 regarding comparative information that relates to annual periods beginning before **1 January 2005** but comparative disclosure is required in relation to accounting policies adopted and the identification of recognised assets, liabilities, income and expense arising from insurance contracts

Future accounting periods – IFRS 17

In May 2017, **IFRS 17** Insurance Contracts was issued by the IASB

IFRS 17 introduces a comprehensive reporting framework for insurance contracts that is intended to result in insurance companies producing financial statements which are **more comparable**, **consistent** and **transparent**

Insurance Contracts

Implementation of IFRS 17 will cause **significant challenges** for **entities** and **auditors** – there will be changes to **profit recognition patterns**, increased **volatility of profit and equity** and **increased options** and **requirements for judgement** to be exercised – **disclosures** should become more **transparent**

Please refer to pages 669 and 670 of the 2019 edition of the Corporate Reporting Study Manual if further detail is required

Intangibles

Suggested mark allocation in an FR question (CR Q2): 4 marks

Definition

An **identifiable** non-monetary asset without physical substance

Must be **separable** or **arise** from contractual or legal rights to be **recognised**

Treatment

There must be **probable** future economic **benefits** that are **attributable to the asset** which will flow to the entity and it must be possible to measure **cost reliably**

Initial recognition should be **at cost**, including **directly attributable** acquisition costs

Exclusions **not** treated as **directly attributable costs**: costs of **introducing** a new product or service including costs of **advertising** and **promotional** activities, costs of **conducting** business in a new location or with a **new class** of customer (including staff **training**) and **administration** and other **general overhead** costs

Amortisation should be charged and recognised in the P&L – look out for **time apportionment** here

State the **year-end** carrying amount after amortisation

Subsequent expenditure is **not** normally recognised

Expenditure to be treated as an expense (i.e. **not** capitalised)

Start-up costs

Training costs

Advertising and promotional costs

Business relocation and reorganisation costs

All **research phase** expenditure such as search costs, design costs and so on

Activities aimed at obtaining new knowledge

Search for, evaluation and final selection of applications of research findings or other knowledge

Search for alternatives for materials, devices, products, processes, systems or services

Formulation, design, evaluation and final selection of possible alternatives for new or improved materials, devices, products, processes, systems or services

Capitalisation of development costs

To be capitalised, **all** the following criteria must be met

Intangibles

Technical feasibility

Intention to use or sell the asset

Ability to **use or sell** the asset

Asset will generate probable future economic **benefit**

Availability of adequate **technical**, **financial** and **other resources** to complete the development and to use or sell the intangible asset

Ability to **measure reliably** the expenditure attributable to the intangible asset during its development

Tip – it takes time to write all of these criteria out – there will **be few or no marks simply for copying out** so try to **pick the criteria which help you show some knowledge of the exam scenario** and **start** with these (see our discussion of inline definition on **page 6**)

Examples of expenditure which would qualify for capitalisation

Design, construction and testing of pre-production or pre-use prototypes and models

Design of tools, jigs, moulds and dies involving new technology

Design, construction and operation of a pilot plant that is not of a scale economically feasible for commercial production

Design, construction and testing of a chosen alternative for new or improved materials, devices, products, processes, systems or services

Specific internally generated intangible assets which cannot be recognised

Internally generated brands, mastheads, publishing titles and customer lists

The reason is that these costs **cannot be identified separately** from the cost of **developing** the **business as a whole**

Intangible assets acquired as part of a business combination

IFRS 3 provides 5 examples of types of intangible which **should** be recognised separately from goodwill

Marketing-related intangible assets such as **trademarks**

Customer-related intangible assets such as **customer lists**

Artistic-related intangible assets such as **motion picture films**

Contract-based intangible assets such as **franchise agreements**

Technology-based intangible assets such as **computer software**

Intangible assets acquired as part of a **business combination** are normally considered to meet the recognition criteria of IAS 38 – the assets should be measured at FV

Intangibles

Amortisation of an intangible

The amortisation charge should reflect the **pattern** in which the asset's future economic benefits are consumed – if such a pattern cannot be predicted reliably, the **straight-line method** should be used

Residual value should be assumed to be **zero unless** a third party is committed to buying the intangible asset **at the end of its useful life** or unless there is an **active market** for that type of asset and it is probable that there will be a market for the asset at the end of its useful life

The amortisation period and method used for an intangible with a **finite** useful life should be reviewed at each year end

Revaluation of an intangible

Revaluation may be allowed if it can be shown that an **active market** exists for the asset – a revaluation model similar to IAS 16 can then be used (i.e. include the revaluation in a Revaluation surplus in the SFP)

Note that an **offer** from another party to buy the asset **could** suggest that an **active market** exists – however, the items traded must be **homogeneous (absolutely identical)**: in most cases, the items will be **different** in **some** way

> Items such as copyrights, publishing rights and film rights have unique sale values so are **not** homogeneous (**no active** market)

> Items such as fishing rights or quotas or taxi cab licences are **identical** so could qualify for revaluation treatment (**active** market)

Interim Financial Reporting

Not mandatory

IAS 34 does **not** make interim financial reporting **mandatory** – however, interim financial reporting is **strongly encouraged**

IAS 34 encourages **publicly-traded** entities to provide an interim financial report for at least the **first 6 months** of their financial year and to make this report available **no later than 60 days** after the **end** of the interim period

The report can either be a **complete** set of financial statements at the interim date complying **in full with IFRSs** or a **condensed** interim financial report prepared in compliance with **IAS 34's** special requirements

Minimum components

Condensed SFP

Condensed SPL and OCI (either as a single statement or as 2 separate statements)

Condensed SoCIE

Condensed SCF

Selected note disclosures

Periods covered

SFP	End of the current interim period and comparative data at the end of the most recent financial year
SPL and OCI	For the current interim period and cumulative data for the current year to date, together with comparative data for the corresponding interim period and cumulative figures for the previous financial year
SCF	Cumulative to the current year to date with comparative cumulative data for the corresponding interim period in the previous financial year
SoCIE	Current interim period and for the year to date, together with comparative data for the corresponding interim period and cumulative figures for the previous financial year

Materiality

Should be assessed in relation to the interim period financial data – should be recognised that interim measurements rely to a greater extent on estimates than annual financial data

Interim Financial Reporting

Recognition and measurement principles

In general, the same recognition and measurement principles should be used in the entity's interim statements as it applies in its annual financial statements (e.g. on assets and accruals)

Revenue items received occasionally, seasonally or cyclically

Should **not** be **anticipated** or **deferred** (accruals or prepayments) in interim financial statements **if** it would be **inappropriate** to anticipate or defer the revenue in the **annual** financial statements

Costs incurred unevenly during the financial year

Again, follow the same principles as in the full annual financial statements

Appropriate to **anticipate** a cost for property rental where the rental is **paid in arrears**

Inappropriate to **anticipate** part of the cost of a major advertising campaign later in the year, for which no expenses have **yet been incurred**

Payroll taxes or insurance contributions paid by employers

In some countries, these amounts are paid **unevenly** during the year, with most amounts paid **earlier** in the year and a small part in the **second half** of the year – in this case, an estimated average annual tax rate for the year can be used rather than the **actual** cash tax paid

This treatment is appropriate because the taxes are assessed on an annual basis

Cost of a planned major periodic maintenance or overhaul

A **planned event** later in the year must **not** be **anticipated** unless there is a **legal** or **constructive obligation** to carry out this work

The fact that such work is carried out **annually** is **not of itself** sufficient to justify **anticipating** the cost

Other planned but irregularly occurring costs

Should **not** be accrued in an interim report – even if they occur regularly and are planned, they are **discretionary**

Year-end bonus

Should **not be provided** for unless there is a **constructive obligation** to pay a year-end bonus (e.g. a contractual obligation or a regular past practice) and the size of the bonus can be reliably measured

Interim Financial Reporting

Holiday pay

If there is an enforceable obligation on the employer then any **unpaid** accumulated holiday pay may be accrued in the interim financial report

Non-monetary intangible assets

Follow the normal principles of IAS 38 – IAS 34 does **not allow** the deferral of cost in the expectation that it will eventually be part of a **non-monetary intangible asset** that has not yet been recognised – such costs should be treated as an **expense** in the interim statement

Depreciation

Should only be charged in an interim statement on non-current assets that have been **acquired**, **not** on non-current assets that **will be acquired** later in the year

Forex gains and losses

Apply the usual principles of IAS 21 with respect to the rates to be used

Tax on income

Apply the estimated **average** annual tax rate for the year based on the **best estimate** of expected profits for the year – this is **appropriate** because **tax** is charged on an **annual** basis and not on interim figures

> Therefore also take into account anticipated tax credits based on annual figures

Losses should **not** be anticipated – charge tax based on the profits made in the period and then if the losses do subsequently happen later then record a **negative tax charge** for that later period as required

Inventories

Apply the **normal IAS 2 principles** – but it is recognised that it will be necessary to rely more heavily on **estimates** for interim reporting than for year-end reporting

NRV should normally be estimated from **selling prices** and **related costs** to complete and dispose of at the interim date

Inventories

Suggested mark allocation in an FR question (CR Q2): 3 marks

Inventories should be held at the **lower** of **cost** and **Net Realisable Value** (**NRV**)

> If it is necessary to **write down** the value of inventories then this amount should be recognised in the **P&L**
>
> NRV must be assessed at the **end of each period** and compared with **cost** – this could result in the **reversal** of all or part of the original write-down

Cost includes the **costs of purchase**, **conversion** and **other costs** involved in bringing the inventories to their present location and condition

> **Fixed production overheads can** be **included** in cost but on the basis of the **normal** capacity of production facilities (taking account of capacity lost through **planned** maintenance)
>
> **Variable production overheads** should be based on the **actual** use of production facilities
>
> Therefore low production or idle plant will not result in a higher fixed overhead allocation to each unit
>
> **Unallocated** overheads must be recognised as an **expense** in the period in which they were incurred
>
> If production is **abnormally high** the fixed production overhead allocated to each unit will be reduced, so avoiding inventories being stated at more than cost

Costs which would not be included in the cost of inventories

Abnormal amounts of wasted materials, labour or other production costs

Storage costs other than costs that are necessary in the production process before a further production stage

Administrative overheads not incurred to bring inventories to their present location and condition

Selling costs

Cost formulae

Only the **FIFO** and **weighted average cost methods** are allowed under IAS 2 – **L**IFO is not aLlowed.

Cost methods

Standard costs – set up to take account of normal levels of raw materials used, labour time etc – these are reviewed and revised on a regular basis

Retail method – often used in the retail industry where there is a large turnover of inventory items with similar profit margins

Investment Property

Suggested mark allocation in an FR question (CR Q2): 4 marks

Treatment

IAS 40 permits 2 **alternative** accounting treatments: the **cost and depreciation model** as under IAS 16 or the **fair value** model specific to IAS 40 – whichever policy is chosen by the entity, it must be applied to **all** of its investment property

Even if the **cost model** is adopted, the FV of investment property must be **disclosed**

Under the **fair value** model any change in the value of the property is recognised in the **P&L**

An entity that chooses the **FV model** should measure **all** of its investment property at **FV** (unless, exceptionally, this cannot be measured reliably, in which case IAS 16 should be used)

Criteria

The property must be held to earn **rental** or **capital appreciation** or **both**, rather than being **used** in the **ordinary course of the business** (i.e. not owner-occupied, unless the owner-occupation is **insignificant** in certain situations – see below)

Recognise the property as an investment property when it is **probable** that the future economic benefits that are associated with the investment property will **flow to the entity** and the **cost** of the investment property can be measured **reliably**

Transaction costs

Recognise only those costs which are **directly attributable** to the investment property such as **professional fees** and **property transfer taxes**

Self-constructed investment property

Property being **self-constructed** or under development for **future use** as an investment property qualifies as an **investment property**

Leases

If held under a **lease** and **classified as an investment property** then it shall be accounted for as if it were a **finance lease**

Entity occupies part of property and leases out the balance

If the 2 portions can be **sold separately or leased separately under a finance lease** then each is accounted for separately as appropriate i.e. one part could be an investment property and the other part(s) could be PPE, or vice versa

Investment Property

If the portions **cannot** be **sold** or **let** separately then the **entire property** can be treated as an investment property if only an **insignificant** portion is **owner-occupied**

Entity supplies services to the lessee of the property

The property is only an investment property if the services are **insignificant** to the **arrangement as a whole**

Property leased to and occupied by a parent, subsidiary or other group company

The property can be an **investment property** in the entity's own accounts but would be **owner-occupied** (not an investment property) from a group perspective

Changes in use

Example	Accounting treatment
Commencement of owner occupation	Start to apply IAS 16 – if FV model was in use when an investment property then treat FV as the deemed cost on transfer
Commencement of development with a view to sale	Reclassify as inventory under IAS 2 – if FV model was in use when an investment property then treat FV as deemed cost
Development with a view to continued letting	Continue to treat as investment property
End of owner occupation with a view to letting out	Start to apply IAS 40 – if FV model will be used under IAS 40 then revalue at the date of change and recognise the difference as a revaluation under IAS 16
Property held as inventory now let out	Start to apply IAS 40 – if FV model will be used under IAS 40 then revalue at the date of change and recognise the difference in profit or loss
Commencement of operating lease to another party	Start to apply IAS 40

Change in use from PPE to investment property

Account for the property under **IAS 16** up to the date of change in use

If the **revaluation model** is used, account for any **difference** between its carrying amount and its fair value at this date in accordance with IAS 16 i.e. recognise a gain in OCI and as a revaluation surplus

Depreciation should **cease** at the date of change in use

From the date of change in use, IAS 40 applies – the entity may apply IAS 40 on either a fair value basis or in line with IAS 16 – always check the entity's specific policy here

If the property is held at **fair value** under IAS 40, any **year end gain** should be debited to the asset account and credited to the P&L for the year

Remember **not to depreciate** the property once it qualifies as an IAS 40 investment property

Investment Property

Fair value

The fair value should reflect **market conditions** at the reporting date – a valuation which reflects **special circumstances** or a buyer who is **not knowledgeable** of local market conditions should not be used

Professional fees

IAS 40 **permits** the inclusion of **certain costs** within the **capitalised** amount of an investment property

Professional fees and installation of new **capital equipment** are likely to be acceptable but inclusion of **relocation costs** would **not** be – relocation costs should be **expensed** in the P&L

Building does not qualify as investment property under IAS 40 – IAS 16 probably applies

If the IAS 40 criteria are failed, remember to briefly state the IAS 16 criteria instead

Remember that the revaluation model can be used under IAS 16 – a revaluation gain is **stored up** in the **revaluation reserve** and recognised in **OCI until sale** rather than hitting the P&L

Depreciation should be charged, reducing the carrying value

Entity occupies the building

The building cannot be an investment property if the entity **occupies** and **uses** a "**significant part**" of the building and the vacant part is not capable of being leased or sold separately – in this case the **whole** building should be treated as a normal owner-occupier building

If the lessor provides services as part of the rental agreement and those services are **more than "insignificant"**, then classification as an investment property is **not** permitted – for example, the lessor could provide basic services such as maintenance and security whilst correctly treating the property as an investment property but if the lessor were to provide **administrative support** or **training services** to the tenant then these would **not** be "insignificant" and the activity would not be investment but rather a form of trading so the property should be treated as owner-occupied

If the entity uses only a **very small proportion** and the rest of the building cannot be sold or leased separately it is acceptable under IAS 40 to treat the **whole building** as investment property

Property is being developed for future sale

Such a building cannot qualify as an investment property – the building must be treated in accordance with IAS 2 until such time as it is **ready for disposal**

Initial recognition should be at **cost** but it should be written down to NRV if this falls below cost

Investment Property

Establishing fair value

IAS 40 states that fair value must be measured in accordance with IFRS 13 which defines fair value as "the price that would be received to sell an asset in an orderly transaction between market participants at the measurement date"

IFRS 13 requires entities to **maximise** the use of **observable** inputs and **minimise** the use of **unobservable** inputs

Level 1 – **quoted** prices in **active markets** for **identical** assets or liabilities

Level 2 – **observable prices other than quoted prices** e.g. quoted prices for **similar** assets **in active markets** or prices for **identical assets in non-active markets**

Level 3 – **unobservable inputs** i.e. models using the entity's own assumptions about market value

In the case of investment properties, a Level 2 input is possible if there are similar buildings being sold in an active market

Downturn in market value

If this has genuinely arisen **after** the year-end, it will be a non-adjusting event after the reporting period and the change in market value should be **disclosed** (rather than **recognised**) in a note to the accounts

If it is possible to measure the value reliably, this value should be used

Audit point

It is generally recommended that the entity should use an external expert in property valuation but IAS 40 does **not require** this

Disclosure points

The entity should disclose

    whether the entity has followed the FV model or cost model

    whether property interests held as operating leases are included in investment property

    criteria for classification as investment property

    assumptions in determining FV

    whether there has been use of an independent professional valuer (encouraged but not required)

    rental income and expenses

    any restrictions or obligations

    if applying the FV model – a reconciliation of the carrying amount of the investment property at the start and end of the period if applying the cost model – depreciation method, rates and useful lives as well as a reconciliation of the carrying amount at the beginning and end of the period – in addition, an entity which adopts the cost model **must disclose the FV** of the investment property even though the FV amount is not used/recognised within the financial statement figures themselves

Joint Arrangements

Suggested mark allocation in an FR question (CR Q2): 4 marks

Joint operation

An arrangement **not structured** through a separate entity is **always** a joint operation – the parties that have joint control (the joint operators) have rights to the **assets** and obligations for the **liabilities** of that joint arrangement

An arrangement structured through a separate entity **could be either** a **joint operation** or a **joint venture**, depending on the rights and obligations of the parties to the arrangement

Each party to the joint operation recognises its **share** of the assets, liabilities, revenue and expenses of the joint operation

Joint venture

Joint control of an entity is split between different parties – **usually** there will be a **separate entity** set up

There is a **contractual arrangement** to share profits and losses and the parties have rights to the **net assets** of the arrangement

Apply the **equity method** – recognise the investment at cost and then add the **share of the joint venture's post-acquisition change in net assets** (**generally** the change in net assets will be caused by the **profits and losses** of the investment) – look out for time apportionment here

The **share** of the joint venture's change in net assets for the year will be recognised in the **P&L**

The investment will be shown as a **non-current asset** in the SFP

An **investor** in a joint venture is a party to the joint venture but which does not have **joint control** over the joint venture – if there is **significant influence** then an Associate exists: if there is no **significant influence** then the accounting should be as a financial asset

Transactions between a venturer and a joint venture

If a venturer sells an asset to the joint venture at a profit and the asset is still held by the joint venture then

> the proportion of the asset that is consolidated **includes an element of profit recorded by the venture**
>
> this amount should be **removed** as it is **unrealised profit**
>
> the remainder will be only the profit that relates to the share of the assets relating to the **other venturers**

If a venturer **purchases** assets **from** the joint venture the venturer's **share of the profit** made by the joint venture should **not be recognised until the asset is sold to a third party**

If a **loss** is made on a transaction between the venture and joint venture then it should be recognised **immediately** if it represents a **reduction** in **realisable value** of current assets or an **impairment loss**

Joint Arrangements

Receivables and payables with the joint venture should **not** be eliminated

Investment to joint operation

An entity may have a previously held interest in a joint operation, held as an investment

A 2017 amendment to IFRS 11 clarified that when an entity obtains joint control of a joint operation it does not re-measure any previously-held interest

Investment to joint venture

In the case of a joint venture previously held as an investment, IFRS 11 requires that a joint venture recognises its interest in a joint venture as an investment in its consolidated financial statements and accounts for that investment using the equity method in accordance with IAS 28

Note that in its separate financial statements, a joint venturer should account for its interest in a joint venture in accordance with IAS 27 *Separate financial statements* i.e. at cost or in accordance with IFRS 9 *Financial instruments* or using the equity method specified in IAS 28

Leases – dealer/manufacturer

Suggested mark allocation in an FR question (CR Q2): 6 marks

Treatment

This treatment applies if the **dealer/manufacturer** makes a sale under a **finance lease**

Recognise a **receivable** equal to the **net investment** in the lease

The seller recognises separately (1) its **normal selling profit** and (2) its **finance income from the lease**, based on **discounting** and then **unwinding** that discount on the cash flows under the lease

Calculate initial **sales revenue** as the **lower** of the **fair value of the asset** and the **present value of the minimum lease payments**, computed at a market interest rate

Calculate **cost of sales** as the **lower** of **cost of production** and **carrying amount less PV of the unguaranteed residual value** – apply this to the initial sales revenue to find the **profit** to be recognised **now**

Calculate **finance income** from the lease – start with the sales revenue figure identified above and deduct any **initial payment made** – then unwind the discount at the applicable interest rate and update the year end net investment in the lease

Split the net investment between receivables falling due within **one year** and receivables falling due **after more than one year** – remember to go **one column to the right of next year's payment** in your lease payment schedule to obtain the amount falling due **after** more than one year – the amount falling due within one year is then a **balancing** amount

Example (amounts in the lease liability table are not exact but purely illustrative)

A dealer sells an item under a finance lease. The FV is £26,250 and the PV of the MLP is £23,000. Purchase price of the item is £21,000. No information on the carrying amount and unguaranteed residual value is available.

Revenue to recognise now is £23,000 and profit to recognise now is £23,000 - £21,000 or £2,000. We also need to recognise some finance income on the finance lease so set up a table with £23,000 (revenue) as the initial figure and then the final year end figure in the table is a receivable to be recognised in the SFP (this can be further split into current and non-current portions if you have time by extending the table by a further year and then looking 1 column to the right of next year's payment)

	b/f	Payment	Capital	Interest	c/f
This year	23,000	(9,000)	14,000	5,000	19,000
Next year	19,000	(9,000)	10,000	4,000	14,000

Receivable of 19,000 can be split into **10,000 non-current** (look at next year's row and then one column to the right of next year's payment) and 9,000 current as a balancing item (again these figures are purely for **illustration**)

Do not forget to mention the **finance income** (P&L) and the **receivable** (SFP) as well as the revenue/profit aspects (P&L) – make sure you state the year-end receivable as updated for finance income and cash received

Leases – finance leases

Suggested mark allocation in an FR question (CR Q2): 6 marks

The IAS 17 factors which would normally indicate that a **lease** is a **finance lease** are as follows

- the lease **transfers** ownership of the asset at the end of the lease term

- the lessee has the **option to purchase** the asset at a price sufficiently below fair value at the option exercise date and it is **reasonably certain** the option will be exercised

- the lease term is for the **major part** of the asset's economic life even if title is not transferred

- the present value of the MLP amounts to **substantially all** of the asset's fair value at inception

- the lessee is responsible for the **insurance** and **maintenance** of the asset

- the leased asset is **so specialised** that it could only be used by the lessee without major modifications being made

- **cancellation** losses are borne by the lessee

- **fluctuations in fair value** at the **end** of the lease accrue to the lessee

- the lessee has an option to extend the lease for a secondary period at a **peppercorn rent** i.e. below market rent

Treatment – lessee's financial statements

Recognise an asset at the **lower** of PV of MLP and fair value

Recognise a corresponding **liability**

Charge a **finance cost** based on the **interest rate implicit** in the lease and recognise this in **finance costs** in profit or loss – look out for **time apportionment**

If the lease is paid **in arrears**, calculate the **interest** based on the **opening figure** for the year

If the lease is paid **in advance**, deduct the cash payments from the **opening figure** for the year **before** calculating interest

Charge **depreciation** based on the initially recognised amount – look out for **time apportionment**

Show the **split** between current and non-current liability (see below)

Cancel out any rental charges if the client has **mistakenly** treated the item as an **operating lease** – there is no rental charge for a finance lease as the lessee is treated as purchasing the item outright over time

If it appears to be **relevant** (use your judgement to determine how many marks there are for the lease as compared to other matters) consider the **cash flow impact** of the lease – **physical cash** payments of **interest** should be recorded in the **SCF** and **repayment** of the **capital element** should be shown as part of "financing activities"

Leases – finance leases

Example finance lease liability tables

Rentals in arrears

	b/f	Interest at 10%	Payment	c/f
This year	24,869	2,487	(10,000)	17,356
Next year	17,356	1,736	(10,000)	9,092

Total lease liability at end of this year is 17,356

Non-current (one column to the right of next year's payment) is 9,092

Therefore the balancing current liability must be 17,356 - 9,092 or 8,264 (i.e. next year's payment net of next year's interest)

Rentals in advance

	b/f	Payment	Capital	Interest at 10%	c/f
This year	34,869	(10,000)	24,869	2,487	27,356
Next year	27,356	(10,000)	17,356	1,736	19,092

Total lease liability at end of this year is 27,356

Non-current (one column to the right of next year's payment) is 17,356

Therefore balancing current liability must be 27,356 - 17,356 or 10,000 (i.e. next year's payment)

Finding the non-current liability

Remember the rule – always look **one column to the right of** next year's payment to find the non-current liability

> Therefore for a lease paid **in arrears** the current liability is equal to the cash payment **net** of next year's interest

> Therefore for a lease paid **in advance** the current liability is equal to the cash payment

Deposits

If an upfront **deposit** is required, deduct this from the **opening liability**

Land and buildings

Originally IAS 17 stated that a lease of land should be treated as an **operating lease** unless title is expected to pass at the end of the lease term

IAS 17 has now been **amended** so in the case of a **long lease** the risks and rewards do pass **regardless of the transfer of title** – therefore a lease of land **can** be a finance lease if it meets the existing criteria

Leases – finance leases

Note that in the FAR Study Manual and FAR past paper model answers a lease of **40** years is considered a **long lease** and the related lease of land was treated as a **finance lease**

Leases – IFRS 16

Note: IFRS 16 will replace IAS 17 with effect from 1 January 2019 – **IAS 17 remains** the **main** standard examinable in Corporate Reporting but candidates are required to have an awareness of IFRS 16 – a considerable amount of content regarding IFRS 16 was added to the 2018 edition of the Corporate Reporting Study Manual and IFRS 16 was then tested in both 2018 past papers so be warned!

General implications of the move to IFRS 16 (based on Corporate Reporting July 2018 past paper Q2)

IFRS 16 replaces IAS 17

The new standard adopts a single accounting model applicable to all leases for lessees – there is no requirement to distinguish between operating and finance leases for lessees

Under IFRS 16, a lease is defined as a contract or a part of a contract that conveys the right to use an asset for a period of time in exchange for consideration

A lessee will need to recognise on its SFP for each lease a right-of-use asset and a corresponding lease liability – this change in treatment could potentially lead to large increases in both the assets and liabilities shown in the SFP

In most cases, the initial amount to be recognised as an asset will be equal to the obligation to make future lease payments (discounted as appropriate) but the asset value will also be adjusted for payments in advance, lease incentives and costs

After initial recognition, the asset will be depreciated over the shorter of its useful life and the lease term – it is this depreciation charge, rather than the operating lease rentals, which will be the cost reflected in the P&L

There may also be impairment charges where a leased asset is impaired

An entity may select 1 of 2 accounting alternatives when first adopting IFRS 16 – it may apply IFRS 16 with full retrospective effect – alternatively, it, as the lessee, is permitted not to restate comparative information but to recognise instead the cumulative effect of initially applying IFRS 16 as an adjustment to opening equity at the date of initial application

Reminder – consider whether there could also be an IFRS 15 issue

We have noticed that many of the past paper answers on IFRS 16 also mention IFRS 15, particularly in relation to sale and leasebacks – IFRS 15 needs to be applied to determine whether a sale has taken place and therefore whether a transfer of rights should be recognised

If a sale has occurred, the selling party will need to calculate the asset value of the rights retained and recognise a gain only on the rights transferred

If the sale proceeds are higher than fair value, the additional proceeds received above fair value will be treated as financing from the buyer

Leases – IFRS 16

Irrelevance of distinction between operating leases and finance leases for lessees

A useful advisory point regarding future accounting periods which would apply to **any** client that currently leases an asset (i.e. is a lessee) under an operating lease or finance lease will be to point out that under IFRS 16 the distinction between operating leases and finance leases ceases to apply for lessees

With the exception of leases for less than 12 months or leases of low value assets, all leases must be recognised in the SFP – this means that there will definitely have to be an SFP entry of some kind for all lessees once IFRS 16 comes into force

A lease liability is recognised, together with a right-of-use, being the lease liability plus (amongst other possibilities) any payment made in advance

Continuing importance of distinction between operating leases and finance leases for lessors

A useful advisory point regarding future accounting periods which would apply to **any** client that currently leases out an asset (i.e. is a lessor) under an operating lease or finance lease will be to point out that under IFRS 16 the distinction between operating leases and finance leases ceases to apply for lessees **but remains applicable to lessors**

Impact of a potential fall in rental income under a lease – interaction with onerous contract rules

In a question which appears to be primarily about an onerous contract (i.e. a situation where the client company no longer needs to lease a property but faces a high penalty charge if the lease is terminated early), look out for a situation where the client can potentially sublet the property but at a reduced rent – as well as the impact of the onerous lease rules, this could also have implications under IFRS 16

Under IFRS 16, the potential fall in rental income indicates that the right-of-use asset is impaired because it is underperforming – an impairment test must be carried out and an impairment loss recognised for the right-of-use asset

Sale and leaseback under IFRS 16

It is correct to say that the treatment of sale and leasebacks will change under IFRS 16

The accounting for sale and leaseback transactions will depend on whether in substance a sale has occurred (i.e. a performance obligation has been satisfied) in accordance with IFRS 15

If the transfer is in substance a sale, the seller-lessee derecognises the asset sold, recognises a right-of-use asset and lease liability relating to the right-of-use retained and a gain/loss in relation to the rights transferred

When the transfer is in substance not a sale, the seller-lessee accounts for the proceeds as a financial liability in accordance with IFRS 9

IFRS 16 – illustration of concept of substitution and economic benefit to the lessor

User Ltd has entered into an arrangement with Provider Ltd regarding the use of certain machinery which will be used to produce car engine parts. Provider Ltd has agreed to provide User Ltd with any one of a selection of 10 similar machines on a weekly basis and has also agreed that the relevant machine must be

Leases – IFRS 16

able to produce 5,000 car parts per day. Provider Ltd can provide User Ltd with any of its 10 similar machines as required at its absolute discretion.

A lease **does not arise** because there is **no identifiable asset** and Provider Ltd (**the lessor**) can **substitute** the machine as it wishes, deriving **economic benefits** from doing so in terms of **convenience**.

User Ltd should account for the rental payments as **a normal expense** in the P&L rather than applying IFRS 16.

IFRS 16 sale and leaseback numerical example – calculation of gain

On 1 July 2018, First Ltd bought a specialised printing machine for £1.2m. The carrying amount on 30 June 2019 was £1.0m.

On 1 July 2019, First Ltd sold the machine to Second Ltd for £1.48m, which was the fair value of the machine. First Ltd immediately leased the machine back for 5 years (the remainder of its useful life) at £320,000 per annum payable in arrears.

The present value of the annual lease payments is £1.4m and the transaction satisfies the IFRS 15 criteria to be recognised as a sale.

Step 1 – calculate the accounting profit on disposal: 1.48m - 1m = 480,000

Step 2 – apply fraction of (PV of leaseback payments / FV of asset): 1.4/1.48 x 480,000 = 454,054

Step 3 – deduct amount found in step 2 from the amount found in Step 1: 480,000 - 454,054 = 25,946

Treat the amount from Step 3 as the gain to recognise immediately.

Note – a shortcut can be applied – the gain to recognise can be calculated simply as 0.08/1.48 x 480,000 = 25,946 – in other words, place the difference between the FV of the asset and the PV of leaseback payments (0.08 in this example) over the FV of the asset and apply this to the accounting profit on disposal – this will be slightly quicker to calculate

Leases – lease incentives

Suggested mark allocation in an FR question (CR Q2): 3 marks

Examples

A **rent-free** period or **reduced rent** on an **introductory** basis

Treatment

Accounted for under **SIC 15 Operating Leases – Incentives**

Recognise the **aggregate benefit** of the incentives as a **reduction** of rental expense **over the lease term**, on a **straight-line** basis

The client accountant will probably have recognised the incentive **upfront** and will therefore have calculated the rental expense for the year on a **cash basis** – this is likely to **understate** the expense as correctly calculated on an accruals basis since the **first year** of expense will be **too low** as **all** of the incentive has been taken **immediately**

It is therefore likely that you will have to **increase the rental expense** and have a corresponding credit to a **payables** account to allow for the missing accrual of rental expense

Calculation

The easiest approach is to find the **total payable** under the lease **excluding** the incentive, find the **total value of the incentive** and deduct this from the **total payable** and then **spread the resulting net amount equally per month** (as there will likely be some **time-apportionment** to consider so having a **monthly** figure will be helpful)

The amount paid in cash is **unlikely** to match the **accounting amount** recognised under SIC 15 so look out for an **accrual** or **prepayment** here and **quantify** this

Example

An entity takes out a 5 year operating lease over a building at an annual cost of £1m per year – the entity agrees a rent-free period of 6 months

The entity should not therefore recognise all of the incentive in the period where this is given in cash terms – for example, in the above example the rent-free period of 6 months should **not** be recognised upfront or all in the first year of the lease but rather the saved costs should be spread equally over the 5 years of the lease

Leases – operating leases

Suggested mark allocation in an FR question (CR Q2): 5 marks

An **operating lease** is any lease that is **not** a **finance lease**

Therefore it is a lease which does **not** transfer **substantially all the risks and rewards** normally associated with **ownership** of an asset

Treatment

No complicated treatment is needed for an operating lease – unlike for a finance lease

Lease expenses should be charged on a **straight-line basis** (unless another systematic and rational basis is more representative of the time patterns of the user's benefit) even if **cash** is not paid on this basis

Therefore look out for an **accrual** or **prepayment** as the cash payments are highly unlikely to match the amounts due under accounting principles

See also our section on lease incentives on **page 143**.

Land and buildings

Originally IAS 17 stated that a lease of land should be treated as an **operating lease** unless title is expected to pass at the end of the lease term

IAS 17 has now been **amended** so in the case of a **long lease** the risks and rewards do pass **regardless of the transfer of title** – therefore a lease of land **can** be a finance lease if it meets the existing criteria

Note that in the FAR Study Manual and FAR past paper model answers a lease of **40** years is considered a **long lease** and the related lease of land was treated as a **finance lease**

Disclosures

Accounting policy for operating leases

Operating lease payments charged as an expense for the period

In respect of non-cancellable operating leases, a commitments note analysed into amounts due within 1 year, within 2 to 5 years and after more than 5 years

> Note that this is not an analysis of liabilities as with a finance lease – it is simply a listing of commitments – there will also by definition be no disclosure of finance charges for operating leases as there are no finance charges applicable to such leases

A general description of **significant** leasing arrangements

Mineral Resources

IFRS 6 deals with expenditures on **exploration for** and **evaluation of** mineral resources but not with **expenditures** incurred **before** the **acquisition** of **legal rights to explore** and **expenditures** incurred **following** the **assessment of technical and commercial feasibility**

Entities may change their policies under IFRS 6 as long as the new information is closer to meeting IAS 8 criteria

IAS 38 applies to the **development** of mineral resources – IFRS 6 only applies to **exploration and evaluation of resources** so it should not be applied when the technical feasibility and commercial viability of extracting a mineral resource are demonstrable

Measurement at recognition

Measure at **cost**, applying expenditure recognition policy consistently

Initially recognised cost may include acquisition of rights to explore, exploratory drilling, sampling, studies and activities relating to commercial evaluation

Record as **tangible** or **intangible assets**, as appropriate

Measurement after recognition

Apply **either** the **cost model** or **revaluation model** under IAS 16

Changes may be made if the change makes the financial statements **more relevant** to users, applying IAS 8 criteria

Impairment

IAS 36 is modified such that impairment tests are required

> When technical and commercial viability of extraction is demonstrable, at which point **IFRS 6 is no longer relevant to the asset**

> When other facts indicate that the **carrying amount exceeds recoverable amounts** such as exploration rights have expired, there has been no success in finding commercially viable mineral resources and the entity has decided to discontinue exploratory activities within a specific area or estimates suggest that the carrying amounts of assets are unlikely to be recovered in full following successful development of the mineral resource

If it is required, impairment testing is undertaken in accordance with IAS 36

Presentation and disclosure

Disclosure involves the **description** of the **accounting policies applied** and the **amounts** relating to assets, liabilities, income and expense as well as operating and investing cash flows arising from exploration for and evaluation of mineral resources

Once benefits are demonstrable, **other standards supersede IFRS 6** and the assets are reclassified accordingly

Onerous Contracts

Suggested mark allocation in an FR question (CR Q2): 3 marks

A contract in which the **unavoidable costs** of meeting the obligation under the contract **exceed** the **economic benefits** expected to be received under it

Unavoidable costs are the **lower** of the **cost** of **fulfilling** the contract and any **penalties** arising from **failing to fulfil** it

This means that the entity must only provide for the **lower** net cost of exiting the contract – this is because a **rational** entity will pick the **lower** cost so that is the **maximum** cost that it could incur and hence it is the amount of the provision

- **Be careful here** – it is **tempting** to use the **higher** figure on the grounds of **prudence** but, as indicated, the entity will not choose that option in practice so it is not a relevant figure

Treatment

The present obligation under the contract should be recognised and measured as a **provision in the SFP**

- A present obligation from a past event exists (a lease was signed)
- An outflow of economic benefit is probable (rentals or a penalty will be payable)
- The amount can be measured reliably (future rentals or the penalty, discounted if discounting would make a material difference to the figure)

The **corresponding amount** should be recognised in the **P&L**

Operating Segments

Suggested mark allocation in an FR question (CR Q2): 2-3 marks

Note – there will not be **many** marks for IFRS 8 issues (unless a detailed numerical working is needed) but the marks that are available can be **obtained very quickly indeed**

Tip – if the question refers to a plc which is undergoing some kind of change (acquisition, disposal, restructuring) then this is probably a hint that there will be a couple of marks for IFRS 8 issues

IFRS 8 – only applicable to publicly traded entities

Only entities whose equity or debt securities are **publicly traded** need to disclose segment information under IFRS 8

In **group** accounts, only **consolidated** segmental information needs to be shown

Operating segment definition

A **component** of an entity that engages in business activities from which it may **earn revenues and incur expenses** (including revenues and expenses relating to transactions with other components of the same entity) …

… whose operating results are **regularly reviewed by the entity's chief operating decision maker** to make decisions about **resources to be allocated** to the segment and assess its performance …

… for which **discrete financial information** is available

The term "**chief operating decision maker**" refers to a function rather than to a manager with a specific title so need not refer to a particular individual

Aggregation

Two or more segments may be aggregated if the segments have **similar economic characteristics** and the segments are similar in **all** the following respects

- Nature of **products or services**
- Nature of the **production process**
- Type or class of **customer** for their products or services
- **Methods** used to **distribute** their products or provide their services
- Nature of the **regulatory environment**

Operating Segments

Threshold for reportability

Determination of **reportable segments** – segment is **reportable** if

It is an operating segment and any of the following size criteria are met:

Segment revenue is at least **10%** of total (internal and external) revenue, or

Segment profit or loss is at least **10%** of the profit of **all** segments in **profit** (or at least 10% of the loss of **all** segments making a **loss,** if greater)*, or

Segment assets are at least **10%** of **total** assets

At least 75% of total external revenue must be reported – if this is not the case based on those segments identified based on the above rules then **additional** segments must be added even if these **do not themselves** meet the 10% thresholds

*For the purposes of this test, look at **all profitable** segments and find **10% of the total profit** – then look separately at **all segments making a loss** and find **10% of the total loss** – do not calculate 10% of any figure which deducts losses from profits

Disclosures – segment-level

Segment disclosures

Factors used to identify the entity's reportable segments

Types of products and services from which each reportable segment derives its revenues

Operating segment **profit or loss, segment assets, segment liabilities, certain income and expense items including a reconciliation**

Disclosures – entity-wide

External revenue by each product and service

Geographical information: external revenue and non-current assets by entity's country of domicile and all foreign countries

Information about **reliance on major customers** which represent **more than 10% of external revenue**

Pension schemes – narrative on different types

Suggested mark allocation in an FR question (CR Q2): 3 marks

Please note: you will not necessarily need the below points in every pensions question – however, sometimes you may be asked to explain the different types of scheme to the client and the notes below should then be used

Defined contribution scheme (employee makes a specified contribution)

Accounting is more straightforward

Risk not reflected in the figures in the SFP – no need to include a liability on the SFP

The employer (and possibly employees) pay regular contributions of a "defined" amount each year

These amounts are invested and the **size of pensions paid to former employees depends on how investments perform**

Employees bear the risk that investments may not perform well

Defined benefit scheme (employer is responsible for providing a specified pension)

Accounting is much more complicated – the **FV of plan assets** and **PV of plan liabilities** must be calculated and disclosed

The size of pension benefits which can be claimed after employment is determined or "defined" in advance

The employer and possibly employees pay contributions into the plan with the size of the contributions set at an amount **expected to earn enough investment returns to meet obligations** to pay post-employment benefits

The entity bears the risk that the funds may be insufficient as the employer will be required to make up the shortfall

If assets are larger than the liability for postemployment benefits, the employer may be allowed to take a "**contribution holiday**"

Therefore if the **employer bears risk** the scheme is very likely to be a "**defined benefit plan**"

Additionally, if the entity bears a risk/has a liability in the case that an employee leaves the company and transfers the pension to another fund, then again the scheme is very likely to be a "defined benefit plan"

Pension schemes – pro formas and disclosures

Suggested mark allocation in an FR question (CR Q2): 6 marks

Typical client error – cash contributions treated as P&L charge

It is very common for the client accountant to treat the **cash contributions** to the plan assets as the accounting entry for the **P&L charge** for the year – this is incorrect as it does not reflect an **accruals** approach

The correcting entry will typically be

Dr Pension plan assets (SFP)

Cr Employee expenses – pensions (P&L)

This will cancel the expense incorrectly recognised by the client on a cash amount (i.e. no net impact on the P&L) whilst moving that payment correctly into the plan assets on the SFP

The 2 pro formas

Note that these pro formas **should not be the whole of your answer** – you also need to write up how the figures calculated in the pro forma are presented in the financial statements i.e. whether they are in the **P&L**, **OCI** or **SFP**

We recommend that you write figures for both pro formas as **positive** figures even for the PV of the obligation – this will reduce confusions with negative numbers and will mean that the benefits paid out to employees claiming a pension will be a **negative** entry in **both** columns (and in most cases the only such negative entry that applies to **both** columns)

We have tried to include **as many possibilities as possible** in the examples below – note that your answer will not necessarily need to use **all** the relevant rows

Change in the FV of plan assets

Fair value of plan assets at [first day of the period]	X
Interest on plan assets (P&L)	X
Cash contributions paid in during the year* (SCF)	X
Benefits paid out during the year (SCF)	(X)
Gain or loss on the re-measurement (OCI)	X/(X)
Fair value of plan assets at [final day of the period]	X

* This figure is likely to have been treated as the P&L charge by the client accountant (see above)

Pension schemes – pro formas and disclosures

Change in the PV of the obligation

Present value of obligation at [first day of the period]	X
Interest cost on obligation (P&L)	X
Current service cost (P&L)	X
Past service cost (P&L) [unusual – see below]	X
Loss or gain on settlement (P&L) [unusual – see below]	X/(X)
Benefits paid out during the year (SCF)	(X)
Gain or loss on the re-measurement (OCI)	X/(X)
Present value of obligation at [final day of the period]	X

Remember to state in your answer where items are recognised in the financial statements – we have included reminders in brackets in the pro-formas above but you will also need to mention this in your answer – subject to time constraints and your estimate of the marks available for the pensions element of the question, consider using the tabular presentation which can be found on the next page

Actuarial gains or losses

These must be recognised in OCI in the year in which they arise

Some double entries

    Retirement benefits paid out

Debit   PV of defined benefit obligation (SFP)

Credit   FV of plan assets (SFP)

    Contributions paid into plan

Debit   FV of plan assets (SFP)

Credit   Cash (SFP)

    Past service cost – increase in obligation

Debit   Past service cost (P&L)

Credit   PV of defined benefit obligation (SFP)

    Past service cost – decrease in obligation

Debit   PV of defined benefit obligation (SFP)

Credit   Past service cost (P&L)

    Gain on settlement

Debit   PV of defined benefit obligation (SFP)

Credit   Past service cost (P&L)

Pension schemes – pro formas and disclosures

Loss on settlement

Debit   Past service cost (P&L)

Credit   PV of defined benefit obligation (SFP)

Discount rate

The discount rate adopted should be the market yield on **high-quality fixed rate corporate bonds** – if there is no "**deep**" market for such bonds, the yields on **comparable government bonds** should be used instead

Past service costs and settlements

These relate to a change in the PV of the defined benefit obligation because of an **amendment** (change in benefits offered by a plan), **curtailment** (reduction in the number of employees covered by the plan) or **settlement** (transaction to eliminate employment benefit obligations)

Past service costs are recognised at the **earlier** of (1) when the plan amendment or curtailment **occurs** and (2) when the entity **recognises** related **restructuring costs** or **termination benefits**

All gains and losses arising from past service costs or settlements must be recognised **immediately** in profit or loss

Full disclosure pro forma

Important: use your judgement here – how many marks are available for pensions as compared to other parts of the question? You **may not need** to present these full disclosures …

At the same time, it is important to note that simply producing the change in the PV of the obligation and change in the FV of plan assets pro forma is not enough (see above) to fully answer the question – you need to indicate to the examiner exactly **how these numbers are disclosed in the financial statements**, either in your narrative write-up or by the presentation of the tables noted below

Amounts recognised in the statement of financial position

	Current year	Prior year
Present value of obligation	X	X
Fair value of plan assets	(X)	(X)
Net liability	X	X

Expense recognised in profit or loss for the year ended XXXX

Current service cost	X
Net interest on the net defined benefit obligation*	(X)
[Other P&L items from the question]	X
Net expense	X

* As the defined benefit obligation will almost certainly exceed the fair value of the plan assets we have assumed that there will be a net interest expense (rather than net income) in the P&L

Amount recognised in other comprehensive income for the year ended XXXX

Actuarial loss on obligation	(X)
Return on plan assets excluding amounts in net interest	X
Net re-measurement loss*	(X)

* As there is almost always an actuarial loss in the question we have assumed that there is a net re-measurement loss here

Performance review – tips

General tips

Watch your **timing** – CR past papers have **not** tended to award a **high number of marks** for performance review (in contrast to the Question Bank questions which sometimes allocate an **entire 30 marks to performance review**) – therefore **do not try to be too ambitious**: there will be many marks available in the question for other areas/topics

Start with a data table – not only does this look good, it ensures that you know what the **big picture** is **before** you start writing – you can always supplement the data table with a few further calculations in brackets mixed into the narrative if you need to

Use plenty of **headings**, ensuring that you are **spreading** your points well and doing everything asked in the question wording – ensure that you refer to at least some extent to each **requirement** of the question – **do not write too much on the Income Statement** just because this is the **first part** of the question, for example

Focus on the **bigger movements** and the **movements which can be explained from the scenario** – the examiner does not care if inventory days have moved from 46.3 to 46.7, particularly if there is nothing in the Exhibit information to explain this

Apply some **professional scepticism**, especially if **forecasts** are involved – there will **always** be **more information that you would like to have**

Look out for the **context** of the scenario – does this give **management** an incentive to be **unrealistic**? e.g. if the information is prepared for a bank as part of restructuring or to apply for a loan, might this give a reason for unrealistic predictions?

Consider **further information** that may be needed – look for ratios that you would **like to calculate** but cannot calculate based on the figures – look for **contingent liabilities** or indications that asset values may differ under a FV approach

Think about the **user** of the report – a bank will want to see a good stream of **earnings** and **good interest cover** to repay interest and loan capital, an investor will want to know **dividend yield** and recent **EPS** figures

Again, remember that the **past exam papers** have **not** given **as many marks** for the performance review as the **example questions in the Question Bank** which are dedicated solely to performance review – do not go **overboard** with your CR review (**particularly if you are also doing SBM** – there will almost certainly be more marks in SBM for performance review)

Make **scenario-specific** points – explain the figures based on the scenario and suggested causes – do not just write in a load of numbers and changes **with no explanation**

Create **scenario-specific indicators** – revenue per store or per employee or gross profit per car etc will always be more interesting for the reader than "**standard**" points such as **revenue increase** or **gross profit margin** – **try not just to use indicators that could be used in any question**

Further information points – add a few areas where **further information** would be useful but try to avoid **generic** points – make points that are **specific to the scenario** – try not have **too many further information points or you will run out of time quickly**

Try to offer a brief **conclusion** section under an appropriate heading

Performance review – tips

Profitability

Consider ratios such as margins, return on equity, return on capital employed

Try to use **scenario-specific indicators** – gross profit per shop (etc) so that your answer is **not generic**

Liquidity

Consider using ratios such as the current ratio, quick ratio, receivables days, payables days, inventory days

Look out for any need to pro-rate the assessment e.g. if assessing the 6 monthly accounts then use 180 days not 365 days for the working capital days ratios

Cash generation

Consider explaining why there is a difference between accounting profit/loss and cash generation

Further information example – general reminders – remember to add scenario specific content

Further analysis of revenue

Figures adjusted for exceptionals to understand true like-for-like changes

Geographical or segmental data such as locations of new offices or openings

Non-current asset disclosure information to understand depreciation policies and to make comparisons with industry averages – analysis of capital expenditure

Information on dividend policy

Details of future plans and management initiatives

Information on employees and employee numbers

Further detail on key cost categories

Details of the tax charge

Details of potential diluting financial instruments that could affect DEPS

Further information example – contingent liability

Report from the investigation into the issue to understand the likelihood of having to pay out on the issue and any monetary sums that may have to be paid

Information on whether a write-down of any items is needed

Information on press reporting of the issue to understand reputational damage

Post year-end information to determine the potential future impact of the issue

Whether safeguards have been put in place to prevent the issue happening again

Details of relevant contracts to assess profitability and operational requirements

© ACA Simplified 2019. No copying or reproduction permitted.

Performance review – ratios

Important notice: do not spend too long on the numbers – **choose only the most relevant ratios**

Always start by first using the scenario-specific indicators given in the question (e.g. the client's own internal performance metrics) and only move onto these more "generic" analysis points **after** the scenario-specific indicators have been thoroughly used.

Performance ratios

$$gross\ profit\ margin = \frac{gross\ profit}{revenue} \times 100\%$$

Replace gross profit with **operating profit to get operating profit margin**. This allows you to see whether cost of sales (gross profit) or admin costs (net profit) are more significant as a constraint on returns

$$return\ on\ capital\ employed\ [ROCE] = \frac{PBIT + associate's\ post\ tax\ earnings}{equity + net\ debt}$$

Net debt = interest-bearing debt (current and non-current) less cash and cash equivalents

Equity = exclude redeemable preference shares, in line with general treatment as a loan, not equity

$$return\ on\ equity\ [ROE] = \frac{profit\ before\ tax}{equity\ or\ net\ assets} \times 100\%$$

Note that ROE is quicker to calculate than ROCE and with less chance of error

$$return\ on\ shareholders'\ funds\ [ROSF] = \frac{profit\ attributable\ to\ owners\ of\ parent}{equity\ less\ NCI}$$

Profit attributable to owners of parent will usually be profit after tax

Note the difference: ROCE uses profit **before** tax; ROSF uses profit **after** tax

You can remember this by thinking of ROSF as measure of what the shareholders get i.e. after tax, whereas ROCE is more of a measure of the capacity of the business to generate a return, and tax is then a subsequent cost to be considered later

Exam tip – ROSF is usually quicker and easier to calculate, saving valuable time – you can then comment that ROSF only looks at equity as a source of resources to pick up marks for scepticism as well

Liquidity ratios

$$current\ ratio = \frac{current\ assets}{current\ liabilities}$$

Usually expressed as a multiple e.g. 3:1 (equivalent to 6/2)

Performance review – ratios

$$\text{quick ratio} = \frac{\text{current assets less inventories}}{\text{current liabilities}}$$

Basically, the current ratio adjusted for inventories as these cannot be turned into cash very **quickly**.

Long-term solvency ratios

$$\text{gearing} = \frac{\text{net debt as per ROCE}}{\text{equity as per ROCE}} \times 100\% \text{ or gearing} = \frac{\text{net debt}}{\text{net debt} + \text{equity}} \times 100\%$$

$$\text{interest cover} = \frac{\text{PBIT plus investment income}}{\text{interest payable}}$$

Efficiency ratios

$$\text{net asset turnover} = \frac{\text{revenue}}{\text{capital employed}}$$

$$\text{receivables period} = \frac{\text{trade receivables}}{\text{revenue}} \times 365 \text{ days}$$

$$\text{payables period} = \frac{\text{trade payables}}{\text{cost of sales}} \times 365 \text{ days}$$

Strictly, use credit purchases but usually you will have to use cost of sales

Investor ratios

$$\text{dividend cover} = \frac{\text{earnings per share}}{\text{dividend per share}}$$

$$\text{price earnings ratio} = \frac{\text{market price per share}}{\text{earnings per share}}$$

Other ratios

$$\text{CAPEX to depreciation} = \frac{\text{capital expenditure (CAPEX)}}{\text{depreciation}}$$

Measures whether new expenditure compensates for depreciation.

$$\text{non} - \text{current asset ageing} = \frac{\text{accumulated depreciation}}{\text{non} - \text{current assets at cost}}$$

Allows an estimate of how far non-current assets are through their working lives e.g. if depreciation is £2m and the assets cost £4m, then we are 2/4 = 50% through their working lives.

Note: the above 2 ratios require data on depreciation. Hence they are subject to the depreciation method/charge decided upon by management (i.e. subjective).

$$\text{dividend yield} = \frac{\text{dividend per share}}{\text{current market price per share}} \times 100\%$$

Performance review – ratios

Cash flow ratios

Least likely to be possible to calculate in CR or SBM but included for completeness

Note: the concept of "cash return" is important here and is used in several ratios

cash return = cash generated from operations + interest received + dividends received

$$cash\ ROCE = \frac{cash\ return}{capital\ employed\ as\ per\ ROCE} \times 100\%$$

$$cash\ from\ operations\ as\ \%\ of\ profit\ from\ operations = \frac{cash\ generated\ from\ operations}{profit\ from\ operations} \times 100\%$$

$$cash\ interest\ cover = \frac{cash\ return}{interest\ paid}$$

$$cash\ flow\ per\ share = \frac{cash\ return - interest\ paid - tax\ paid}{number\ of\ ordinary\ shares}$$

$$cash\ dividend\ cover = \frac{cash\ return - interest\ paid - tax\ paid}{equity\ dividends\ paid}$$

Only look at equity dividends.

The result of (cash return – interest paid – tax paid) is also known as "cash flow for ordinary shareholders".

Provisions

Suggested mark allocation in an FR question (CR Q2): 4 marks

Criteria for recognition

Present obligation as a result of a **past** event

Probable outflow of resources

Amount can be **reliably estimated**

Make sure you **apply these to the scenario** by using **examples** from the examination paper

Discounting

If the impact of time value would be **material**, then the provision should be **discounted** – if the provision amount relates to an **asset** (e.g. machinery) then it should be **added to the cost of that asset**, increasing the depreciation charge over the lifetime of the asset by (discounted amount / life of the asset)

Remember to mention **unwinding of the discount** which creates a **finance cost** and look out for **time apportionment**

Remember to add the **unwound** amount to the **provision** (Dr Finance costs, Cr Provisions) and state the **year end amount**, taking into account the unwound interest to state the **year end liability**

Indicate whether this is a **current or non-current liability** (generally it will be non-current if discounting has been applied because we are looking at an event some time into the future)

The **discount rate** to use will **normally be given** in the question – it should be a rate which reflects **current market assessments** of the time value of money and the **risks specific to the liability** (risk-adjusted rate) or the entity could use a risk-free rate and adjust the cash flows for risk – **risk must not be double-counted**

Onerous contracts (see also page 147)

If future benefits are expected to be less than unavoidable costs the contract is onerous

Excess unavoidable costs should be provided for at the time a contract becomes onerous

Restructuring costs

A constructive obligation arises where there has been a **detailed formal plan** regarding the employees affected and an announcement has been made to those who will be affected

Redundancy costs

Only provide for these if a formal announcement has been made

Provisions

If the client has **mistakenly** created a provision then the correcting journal is likely to be

Dr Provisions (SFP)

Cr Staff expenses/Reorganisation costs (P&L)

Future costs

There must be a **past** obligating event for a **provision** to exist

Example: the costs of fitting smoke filters to comply with future legislation would **not** create a provision as there is no **past obligating** event but it would be correct to provide for the best estimate of fines for non-compliance which are likely to be imposed – in other words, whilst it would be economically and legally sensible for the company to install the filters, it is not actually obliged to do so whereas its actions have created a legal problem and it has thus become obligated to pay the relevant fines

Reimbursement from a third party

Normally this should be held **separately** from the provision

A reimbursement should only be recognised when it is **virtually certain** an amount will be received

Recognition and disclosure

A **full reconciliation** of **movements** in provisions should be presented – **detailed narrative explanation** should also be provided – the narrative should include an **estimate** of the financial amount in relation to contingent liabilities and assets as well as indications of uncertainties

Any **increase in the value of the discounted amount** arising from the **passage of time** or the **effect** of any **change in the discount rate** should be **disclosed**

Disclosure may be avoided if this would be **seriously prejudicial** to the position of the entity in dispute with other parties – however, this should only be employed in **extremely rare cases** – details of the **general** nature of the provision/contingent must still be provided, together with an explanation of **why** it has not been disclosed

Contingent liability – definition

A **past event** may lead to a liability in future but this will only be **confirmed** by the outcome of **some future event not wholly within the entity's control,** or **payment is not probable**, or the amount of payment cannot be **measured reliably**

A contingent liability is **disclosed** rather than recognised in the financial statements (unless the outflow of resources is thought to be **remote** in which case it is not even disclosed)

Regulatory Deferral Accounts

Applicability

IFRS 14 was issued in January 2014 and is effective for an entity's first annual IFRS financial statements for a period beginning on or after 1 January 2016

Applies to **first-time adopters of IFRS** that provide **goods or services to customers at a price or rate that is subject to rate regulation by the government** e.g. supply of gas or electricity

Need for IFRS 14

Given government **regulation** of prices, the prices charged to customers at a particular time do not necessarily **cover the costs** incurred by the supplier at that time – in this case the recovery of such costs is **deferred** and they are recognised though **future sales**

This leads to a **mismatch** – IFRS does not have specific requirements but practice is normally to recognise these amounts in the P&L as they arise

> However, local **GAAP in some countries** allows such activities to be recovered via a **separate regulatory deferral account** or **as part of the cost of a related asset** – IFRS 14 allows **first-time adopters of IFRS** to **continue** to recognise amounts related to rate regulation in accordance with their **previous GAAP** when they adopt IFRS via a **special exemption from IAS 8**

An entity **may change** its policy for regulatory deferral accounts **in accordance with IAS 8** but only if the change makes the financial statements **more relevant** and **reliable** to users

Presentation

The amounts of regulatory deferral account balances are **separately presented** in an entity's financial statements

Disclosures

Disclosures should be made to **enable users** to assess the **nature of, and risks associated with, the rate regulation that establishes the price(s) the entity can charge customers** for the goods or services it provides as well as the effects of rate regulation on the entity's financial statements

Related Party Transactions

Suggested mark allocation in an FR question (CR Q2): 3-4 marks

Signposts

Director **controls** one company and is in a position to **control or significantly influence a second company** which has some kind of **dealings with the first company** – this means that an entity is controlled by one of the key **management personnel** of another entity so the 2 entities are **related parties**

Contract terms not as standard e.g. a receivable with credit terms of 12 months

Look out for one of the entities being in **financial difficulties** – consideration should then be given to making an allowance for the debt and this would need to be **disclosed**

Definitions

A **person or close member of that person's family** is related to a reporting entity if that person

> has control or joint control over the reporting entity
>
> has significant influence over the reporting entity or
>
> is a **member of the key management personnel of the reporting entity** or of a parent of the reporting entity*

An **entity is related to a reporting entity** if

> the entity and reporting entity are members of the same group
>
> one entity is an associate or joint venture of the other entity
>
> both entities are joint ventures of the same third party
>
> one entity is a joint venture of a third entity and the other entity is an associate of the third entity
>
> the entity is a post-employment benefit plan for the benefit of employees of either the reporting entity or of an entity related to the reporting entity
>
> the entity is controlled or jointly controlled by a person identified under the first set of rules above (rules relating to a person or close member of that person's family)*
>
> a person with control or joint control over the reporting entity has significant influence over the entity or is a member of the key management personnel of the entity or of a parent of the entity

*Notice how these rules **interact**: a member of the key management personnel of the reporting entity is a related party of that entity and IAS 24 then says that if that individual controls another entity then that entity becomes a related party of the reporting entity (being a member of key management personnel whilst controlling another entity creates a **link** here)

Close members of the family of a person include that person's children and spouse or domestic partner, children of that person's spouse or domestic partner and dependants of that person or that person's spouse or domestic partner

Related Party Transactions

Key management personnel

A member of **key management** of an entity is a **related party of that entity** – this includes Non-Executive Directors

Therefore the sale of company property to a marketing director (for example) would be a related party transaction

Not related parties

Two entities **just because** they have a director or member of key management personnel **in common** or **just because** a member of the key management personnel of one entity has significant influence over the other entity (it is, however, necessary to consider how that director would affect both parties)

Two venturers simply because they share joint control over a joint venture

Providers of finance, trade unions, public utilities and government departments that do not control, jointly control or significantly influence the reporting entity simply by virtue of their normal dealings with an entity

A customer, supplier, distributor etc who transacts a significant volume of business with the entity – there may be some economic dependence here but that is not sufficient to create a related party situation

Treatment

The existence of any relevant balances should be **disclosed** in the notes to the financial statements – **full disclosures** should be made **even if transactions took place on an arm's-length basis**

The fact that the transactions took place on an arm's-length basis may be disclosed but only if such terms can be **substantiated**

There should be disclosure of

- the **nature** of the relationship
- the **amount** of the transactions
- the **amount** of any **balances** outstanding at year-end
- any **provision** against outstanding balances and the expense recognised for bad and doubtful debts due from related parties
- any special terms and conditions attached to the balance

Note that there is no requirement to identify related parties by **name**

Transactions in relation to those balances should also be **disclosed** – for example, if there is a write-off of a loan to a director

It may be worth noting that the tax implications of such a transaction should also be considered, especially if it involves a foreign jurisdiction

Note that being **immaterial** is **not** an excuse to fail to disclose a related party transaction – the nature of related party transactions is that they are material by **nature**, rather than by **value**

Group scenarios

RPTs and outstanding balances with other entities in a group **are disclosed** in an **individual** entity's financial statements – these balances will be eliminated on consolidation in the financial statements of the **group** and are **not disclosed**

Research & Development

Suggested mark allocation in an FR question (CR Q2): 5-6 marks

Research phase (expense)

Treat as an **expense** as incurred – in this period there is **insufficient evidence** that the expenditure will generate **future** economic **benefits**

Investigation work will count as an **expense**

Development phase (capitalise)

Must meet strict criteria

- **technical feasibility** of completing the asset
- **intention** to complete the asset
- **ability** to use the asset
- demonstration of the **commercial viability** of the asset
- availability of **adequate resources**
- reliable measurement of expenditure

Tip – it takes time to write all of these criteria out – there will **be few or no marks simply for copying out** so try to **pick the criteria which help you show some knowledge of the exam scenario** and **start** with these (see our discussion of inline definition on **page 6**)

Capitalise from the date that all the criteria are met

Amortisation should **start** when the asset is **available for use** – note that this may be later than the time when the item is advertised/promoted/marketed: it must be available to be **used**

- If there is a gap between such dates, consider whether an **impairment review** is needed to ensure that the recoverable amount is not less than the carrying amount

Items not to capitalise (even after the criteria have been met)

Launch activities – such activities do not involve design, construction or testing and so should be expensed when incurred

Possible deferred revenue?

If payment has been made for some form of development to be delivered to the customer and the asset has not yet become ready to use, any payments already made by the customer will effectively be deposits as risks and rewards have not been transferred

Research & Development

These amounts must not be recognised as revenue but instead must be held as deferred income as part of current liabilities (assuming that the item will be delivered in the next accounting period: if not, then a non-current liability may be appropriate)

Revenue Recognition – IFRS 15

Note – please check our disclaimer stated on **page 12** of this book for an explanation of how the notes in this section have been compiled

Steps in the 5 step IFRS 15 revenue recognition process

Identification of the contract with the client

Identification of the separate performance obligations in the contract

Determination of the price (the total payable for all elements included in the initial contractual arrangement – this may be a complex determination where, for example, discounts are offered for future years)

Allocate the transaction price between the performance obligations based on the stand-alone prices for each element

Recognise revenue when or as the performance obligations are satisfied (this is likely to be at a single point in time for goods but over time in the case of services)

Delivery date as the normal date for satisfaction of the performance obligation in relation to a sale of goods

Under IFRS 15, revenue should be recognised for the sale of goods when the entity satisfies the relevant performance obligation, which is when control is passed to the customer

This would normally occur on the passing of possession of the goods i.e. physical delivery

However, note that there could be special circumstances such as bill and hold sales (see notes below) where different rules apply

Impact of an order for physical products being non-cancellable

It is not correct for the entity to recognise revenue in the year simply because orders for a physical product cannot be cancelled

Under IFRS 15, revenue should only be recognised when the performance obligations in the contract have been satisfied

The performance obligation is likely to be the supply of the physical product which will be satisfied when control of the product has been transferred to the buyer, which is normally upon delivery

Any cash received in relation to orders not yet fulfilled should be treated as a contract liability (deferred revenue), even if the order is non-cancellable

Installation date as date of satisfaction of the performance obligation

If it requires time to install a physical product then, under IFRS 15, revenue should not be recognised until the installation is complete and the performance obligation has therefore been satisfied

Revenue Recognition – IFRS 15

Construction of an asset which requires a significant period to build

Note that such contracts were previously dealt with under specific IAS 18 rules on "construction contracts" but IFRS 15 does not have any such special treatment and instead deals with such contracts under its general rules on contracts whose performance obligation is satisfied "over time"

As a contractor, the entity should account for the construction of this type of asset in accordance with IFRS 15

It is likely to be a contract in which the performance obligation is satisfied "over time" because the contract meets the following IFRS 15 criteria (subject to the specific circumstances in your examination question so please check and quote the relevant question Exhibit material as required):

- the entity's performance creates or enhances an asset that the customer controls as the asset is created or enhanced

- the entity's performance does not create an asset with an alternative use to the entity and the entity has an enforceable right to payment for performance completed to date

- for a performance obligation satisfied "over time", IFRS 15 states that revenue should be recognised by measuring progress towards complete satisfaction of that performance obligation

Appropriate methods of measuring progress include output methods and input methods

An appropriate output method allowed by IFRS 15 is "surveys of performance completed to date", often referred to in the construction industry as "work certified" – this method is less subjective since it does not rely on estimates of future costs to calculate the percentage complete

An appropriate input method allowed by IFRS 15 is costs incurred – this will require a subjective estimate of future costs to complete so that the completion to date can be assessed as a percentage of total costs

The choice of method could affect the periods in which profit is recognised but the total profit recognised should be the same under any method

In the SFP, gross amounts due from customers should be presented as contract costs incurred plus recognised profits less invoices raised to customers – trade receivables should include the amount invoiced less amounts received from the customer

Treatment as a performance obligation which is satisfied "over time" under IFRS 15

IFRS 15 states that an entity transfers control of the good or service "over time" and therefore satisfies a performance obligation and recognises revenue over time if any of the following criteria are met:

- the customer simultaneously receives and consumes the benefits provided by the entity's performance as the entity performs

- the entity's performance creates or enhances an asset (e.g. work in progress) that the customer controls as the asset is created or enhanced, or

- The entity's performance does not create an asset with an alternative use to the entity and the entity has an enforceable right to payment for performance completed to date

Revenue Recognition – IFRS 15

Bundling of a product and related maintenance services contract

In such a situation, it is possible that 2 different performance obligations can be identified – the supply of the physical product and, secondly, a related ongoing maintenance contract

Under IFRS 15, the transaction price is allocated to each performance obligation (which will impact on when revenue in relation to each part of the bundle can be recognised) in proportion to the relative stand-alone selling price of the goods or services provided within each performance obligation

If the entity sells products and a maintenance contract separately, it will have good evidence of stand-alone selling prices by reference to what customers pay separately for those items so it is likely that IFRS 15 would require such information to be used in determining the correct allocation and recognition of revenue

Supply of the physical item is likely to be a performance obligation satisfied at a point in time – such a performance obligation is satisfied when control of the item or items has been transferred to the buyer, which is normally at the time of delivery

Supply of the related maintenance contract is likely to be a performance obligation satisfied "over time" because the customer simultaneously receives and consumes the benefits provided by the entity's performance as it performs

Time elapsed (an input method) is an appropriate way to measure progress toward satisfaction of the performance obligation and therefore revenue on the maintenance services contract should be recognised over the relevant time period of that contract

Property management services contract

Under IFRS 15, revenue should be recognised when, or as, a performance obligation is satisfied

The performance obligation in a property management services contract is the provision of those services (a contract in which the performance obligation is satisfied "over time")

If a deposit has been received in advance of the services being provided then no amount of revenue should be recognised on the deposit as performance has not been satisfied

Instead, the deposit amount is a contract liability (deferred revenue) which is defined by IFRS 15 as "an entity's obligation to transfer goods or services to a customer for which the entity has received consideration (or the amount is due) from the customer"

Interaction with IFRS 16 in the case of a sale and leaseback

To constitute a genuine sale, a sale and leaseback transaction will need to meet the criteria of IFRS 15

If the criteria are met, the asset sold is derecognised and a right-of-use asset is recognised together with a lease liability relating to the right-of-use retained and a gain/loss in relation to the rights transferred

Revenue Recognition – IFRS 15

Bill and hold sales

When the buyer requests that the delivery of goods purchased does not take place immediately even though the buyer takes legal title of the goods and pays for them, such arrangements are commonly referred to as "bill and hold" sales

Under IFRS 15, revenue from such sales should be recognised when the buyer takes title to the goods provided that:

- the reason for the bill and hold arrangement must be substantive (e.g. the customer has requested the arrangements)

- the product must be identified separately as belonging to the customer (e.g. it is stored in a separate storage area)

- the product currently must be ready for physical transfer to the customer (e.g. the product has been completed and is ready for delivery)

- the entity cannot have the ability to use the product or to direct it to another customer (e.g. the product has been made to an exclusive design for the particular customer in question)

If a bill and hold sale appears to have taken place under IFRS 15 the goods must be removed from closing inventories in the SFP at their cost with a corresponding increase in cost of sales and revenue (and profit) must be recognised in the P&L for the year

Reward cards and loyalty points

Reward or loyalty points provide a material right to customers that they would not receive without entering into a contract

Therefore, the promise to provide goods and services to the customer in exchange for points is a performance obligation under IFRS 15

The total revenue received must be apportioned between the underlying sales and the related reward points, based on stand-alone prices

The allocation should also take into account the likelihood of customers actually claiming the points – for example, if there are total reward points with a face value of £5 million at the year-end but only 2 in 5 customers are expected to actually redeem their points then the value of the points should be calculated as £2 million (i.e. £5m x 2 / 5)

Once the correct value of the reward points (taking into account the probability of actual claim) has been calculated, this should be added to the revenue on the underlying sales for apportionment purposes – for example, if there is total underlying revenue of £100 million on equipment sales plus £2m of loyalty point value (taking into account the probability of actual claim) then the allocation would be as follows:

Equipment sales	100 / 102 x 100	98.04
Loyalty points	2 / 102 x 100	1.96
		100.00

In substance, customers are implicitly paying for the reward points they receive when they buy other goods and services and hence some of the total revenue should be allocated to the points as a separate performance obligation

Revenue Recognition – IFRS 15

In the above example, £98.04 million would be recognised as revenue for the year and the balance of £1.96 million would be recognised as a contract liability (deferred revenue) in the SFP until the reward points are actually redeemed

Treatment of costs incurred in relation to satisfied or partially satisfied performance obligations

IFRS 15 requires that costs incurred in relation to satisfied or partially satisfied performance obligations (i.e. costs related to past performance) must be expensed as they are incurred

Therefore, once a performance obligation starts being performed, the costs will be written off to the P&L as they are incurred

Treatment of direct costs incurred prior to the point at which the performance obligation on a service is met

Direct costs incurred prior to the point in time at which the performance obligation on a service is met must be expensed as incurred under IFRS 15 and may not be carried as work in progress – however, the incremental costs of obtaining a contract (such as sales commission) are recognised as an asset if the entity expects to recover those costs

Rights Issue

Suggested mark allocation in an FR question (CR Q2): 4 marks

Explanation

A rights issue provides current shareholders with newly-issued shares in proportion to their existing holdings at a discount to the market price

Given the discount, a rights issue is in effect a combination of an issue at full market value and a bonus issue

An adjustment factor is therefore calculated to allow for the bonus element

This fraction is defined as **current market price / TERP** (calculated as explained below)

Only apply this fraction to the period **before** the rights issue – after the rights issue has taken place there is no need to apply the fraction: just increase the **total number of shares** to allow for the rights issue

Calculation of the TERP adjustment factor

Essentially, you are finding the average price under the **rights issue** – this is composed of a certain number of shares at the **current** market price plus **additional** shares (normally just 1 additional share) at the **price in the rights issue**

Find the total value of the existing shares at the market value plus the cost of the rights issue and divide this by the number of shares including the rights issue (so if the issue is 1 for 3 then divide by 4)

Then create a fraction based on the current market price / average price just calculated

Example

1 for 3 rights issue at 132p when the market price is 220p

Existing	3	220	660
Rights share	1	132	132
	4		792

TERP is 792 / 4 or 198p

TERP fraction is therefore 220 / 198

> Always have the **higher** figure (**existing market price**) on the **top** of the fraction and the **lower** figure (the **TERP**) on the bottom – the TERP is a lower figure as it is an average of a set of shares which includes rights issue shares issued at **below** the existing market price – therefore, the TERP has to average out at **below** the existing market price

Tip – quoting of the rights issue – "new for old"

Make sure you get the numbers of shares the right way round – the order in which the figures are quoted is based on a "new for old" basis

Therefore, a "1 for 3" rights issue means you will receive 1 new share for every 3 old or existing shares that you already have

Sale and Finance Leaseback

Suggested mark allocation in an FR question (CR Q2): 6 marks

This is essentially a **financing** arrangement – the entity is **not really disposing** of the asset because it is immediately **leased back** under a finance lease under which the entity gradually **buys back the asset** – the entity has maintained the **risks and rewards** of ownership **throughout** this entire process so there is no real sale

However, any profit earned is **deferred** over the lease term so that the overall impact of depreciation on the P&L each year is an amount equal to the depreciation expense **before** the leaseback transaction

Treatment

Derecognise the carrying amount of the asset now sold

Recognise the sales proceeds

Calculate the profit on sale as proceeds less carrying amount and recognise it as **deferred income** over the lease term

Recognise the finance lease asset and the associated liability and measure them in the normal way (at the lower of FV and the PV of MLP)

Impairment

If the **carrying amount** exceeds **fair value** then the asset should be written down to FV **before** the sale and leaseback and the **loss** recognised as an **impairment loss**

Sale and Operating Leaseback

Suggested mark allocation in an FR question (CR Q2): 6 marks

Signposts

The leaseback is for a **small portion** of the **useful economic life** of the asset

Treatment

The substance of the transaction is that of a **sale** – the asset is **sold** by the entity, transferring the risks and rewards of ownership to the other entity, and when it is **immediately leased back** there is **no** transferring back of risks and rewards as using the item under an operating lease **does not mean** the entity is **repurchasing** it

A **profit or loss on disposal** should be recognised **immediately** – however, look out for the need to **defer** some of the gain if the **sale proceeds are above the FV** (as this would not happen in a standard transaction)

> In this case, the **difference** between the **carrying amount and FV** (normal profit) is **recognised immediately** but the unexpected difference between the **proceeds and the FV** is **deferred** and amortised over the **period in which the asset is expected to be used** (normally this will be the length of the lease)

Note that the client has probably recognised the full difference between the **carrying amount and proceeds** as a gain – therefore you will need to **reverse out a portion** (difference between proceeds and FV) and treat this as **deferred income** – then if time apportionment is required (likely) apply our suggested technique to split the deferred income into current and non-current elements

1. Calculate a full year of deferred income – current liability

2. Time apportion the above figure from step 1 as required – current year P&L income

3. The remaining balance (i.e. the total amount minus the figures from step 1 in step 2) must be the non-current liability

Sale and Operating Leaseback

Tabular summary of rules

Sale price at fair value

	Carrying amount equal to FV	Carrying amount below FV	Carrying amount above FV
Profit	No profit	Recognise profit immediately	N/A
Loss	No loss	N/A	Recognise loss immediately

Sale price below fair value

	Carrying amount equal to FV	Carrying amount below FV	Carrying amount above FV
Profit	No profit	Recognise profit immediately	No profit (Note 1)
Loss not compensated for by future lease rentals below market rate	Recognise loss immediately	Recognise loss immediately	(Note 1)
Loss compensated for by future lease rentals below market rate	Defer and amortise loss	Defer and amortise loss	(Note 1)

Sale price above fair value

	Carrying amount equal to FV	Carrying amount below FV	Carrying amount above FV
Profit	Defer and amortise profit	Defer and amortise (Proceeds less fair value) Recognise immediately (FV less carrying amount)	Defer and amortise profit (Note 2)
Loss	No loss	No loss	(Note 1)

Note 1

Carrying amount must be written down to FV with an accompanying impairment loss before the sale and leaseback is accounted for

Note 2

Profit is the difference between FV and sale price because the carrying amount would have been written down to FV

Sale and Repurchase

Suggested mark allocation in an FR question (CR Q2): 3 marks

In this situation, an entity **sells** an asset but has the **right** to repurchase at a particular price at a **later date**

Legal title passes but the arrangement may in **substance** be a **loan** as the entity is receiving money now and will repay this later whilst maintaining ownership of the asset throughout the period

If the repurchase is at a price **below the current market price** then this adds weight to the conclusion that the sale is not a **genuine sale**

Treatment

Revenue should **not** be **recognised** as there is **no genuine sale**

Therefore **profit** should **not be recognised either** – the profit recognised was probably calculated as proceeds less carrying amount so this needs to be reversed

Set up a **loan account** equal to the **proceeds** and charge a **finance cost** based on the **applicable interest rate** (should be given in the question)

Update the **loan receivable** at the year-end for the **accrued interest** based on the loan value at the interest rate (look out for the **time apportionment**) – state the **year end loan balance** and indicate whether this is a **current** or **non-current** liability

Share-based payment – cash-settled

Suggested mark allocation in an FR question (CR Q2): 6 marks

A **cash-settled** share-based scheme makes a payment of **cash** to the employee based on the value of the entity's equity instruments – the employee does not receive any **shares** but rather the **cash value** of those shares – **make sure this is stated in your answer**

Treatment

Recognise an expense over the period that the related services are provided – for example, straight line over 3 years if the employee is required to work for 3 years before settlement of the incentive

The expense is based on the FV of the options – for a cash-settled scheme (and not for an equity-settled scheme) you should take into account changes in the FV of the options each year

> To find this year's charge, use the latest available FV but then look back to see what was already charged – do not go back and change any prior figures but deduct amounts already recognised in prior years as an expense or equity when calculating this year's charge

Remember to use a spreading fraction such as 1/3 in year 1 of a 3 year scheme, 2/3 in year 2 of a 3 year scheme, and so on – but then also allow for the amounts recognised in the prior year

Debit employment expenses and Credit a liability account (probably non-current but check) with the expense for the year

> Again, with a cash-settled scheme you use the latest available FV to find the cumulative expense and cumulative credit to liabilities but to find this year's debits and credits you need to deduct off any amounts already recognised in prior years

(This final stage is not necessary with an equity-settled scheme because the FV never changes once the scheme starts so you can just use the same amounts every year if there is no change in the expected number of employees who will exercise their options.)

Typical cash-settled working

400 employees x 100 options per employee x £16 FV this year x 1/3 for year 1 of a 3 year scheme

380 employees x 100 options per employee x £14 FV this year x 2/3 for year 2 of a 3 year scheme

> Expense and liability found by calculating based on a 2/3 fraction and then deducting previously recognised amounts (as per year 1 calculation, in this case)

475 employees x 100 options per employee x £17 FV this year x 3/3 for year 3 of a 3 year scheme

> Expense and liability found by calculating based on a 3/3 fraction and then deducting previously recognised amounts (as per year 1 and 2 calculations, in this case)

Remember that the 2/3 and 3/3 fractions will find the **total** expense and **total** liability of the scheme – deduct any previously recognised amounts to find this year's charge/liability entry

Also always look out for time-apportionment!

See also our section on Share Appreciation Rights starting on **page 185**.

Share-based payment – equity-settled

Suggested mark allocation in an FR question (CR Q2): 6 marks

The **fair value** of the options at the grant date should be treated as an **expense** in the P&L and **spread** over the vesting period, from the grant date until the date the scheme conditions vest

Only allocate an **expense** based on the **number of employees expected to be in position** at the date the options **vest** i.e. on the **final day** of the scheme

Make sure you **state in your answer** why the scheme is treated as equity-settled – this is because the employee receives **shares** or **equity**

Typical calculation for an equity-settled scheme (assuming some time apportionment)

Number of options per employee x employees who will qualify x FV at grant date x spreading fraction (e.g. 1/3 to spread over 3 years) x time apportionment (e.g. 9/12)

This amount should be charged to the **P&L** with a corresponding **credit in the SFP to equity** – IFRS 2 does not state **where** in equity this entry should arise but many companies add it to **retained earnings**

Dr Employee expenses (P&L)

Cr Retained earnings (SFP)

If the number of employees expected to qualify does not change then the charge will be the same for all years of the scheme (as changes in the FV of the options are not taken into account, unlike with a cash-settled scheme)

Market-based scheme conditions (share-price based) – ignore

Any condition relating to changes in the entity's **share price** is termed a "**market-based** condition"

This type of condition is completely **ignored** in an equity settled scheme – the **possibility of changes** in the share price and the consequent impact on the fair value of the share option is already built into the **initial fair value** of the option

If the shares or share options **do not ultimately vest** because the condition is not met, any amount **already recognised** in the financial statements **will remain** and **will not be adjusted**

Non-market-based scheme conditions – consider

Any condition which does **not** relate to changes in the entity's **share price** is termed a "non-market-based condition"

This kind of condition **is** taken into account in the case of an equity-settled scheme

There will almost always be **one** such condition i.e. that the employee must **continue to work for the entity at the vesting date**

Share-based payment – equity-settled

If there are other such conditions, **only the number of shares or share options expected to vest** will be accounted for, taking into account **whether** the **condition** is **likely** to be met – on the vesting date, the entity should **revise** the **estimate** based on the number of shares or share options that **do actually vest** – this could mean **cancelling out** some prior year figures

Combination of market- and non-market-based conditions

If a scheme has **both** types of condition attached, the **market conditions should be ignored as normal** so provided that **all** other **non-market** vesting conditions are satisfied then an expense and related credit to equity should be recognised

In other words, the **non-market**-based conditions are the conditions which matter

The amounts recognised each year will therefore have **no connection to movements in the entity's share price**

Modification or repricing of share options e.g. a change in the exercise price

Continue to recognise the original fair value in the normal way – recognise any **increase** in fair value at the modification date by **spreading** this over the **period between the modification date and vesting date**

If the modification occurs **after** the vesting date, the additional fair value is recognised **immediately unless there is an additional service period**, in which case the difference is **spread** over this period

Cancellations and settlements

Immediately charge any remaining fair value not already recognised in profit or loss – the cancellation or settlement therefore **accelerates** the expense and **prevents the entity avoiding it**

If an amount is paid to employees on settlement, this is treated as a **buyback of shares** and should be recognised as a **deduction from equity** – if the amount is **in excess of the fair value** of the equity instruments granted, the **excess** should be **recognised immediately in profit or loss**

Variable vesting date

The calculation should be based on the **best estimate** of when vesting will occur

Vested options not exercised

This is the choice of the **holder** of the equity instruments as an investor – therefore there is **no impact** on the **financial statements** of the **entity**

IFRS 2 does permit a transfer to be made **between reserves** to avoid an amount remaining in a separate equity reserve where no equity instrument will be issued

Share-based payment – equity-settled

Deferred tax

In many jurisdictions, a tax allowable expense is available at the **date of exercise**, measured on the basis of the option's **intrinsic value** on that date i.e. the difference between **market price** of a share and the **exercise price** under the share option scheme

The market price of a share at exercise cannot be known with certainty before exercise so in the deferred tax calculations which are needed in the accounting periods before exercise an **estimate** is made based on **assuming that the share price at the end of the current accounting period will also be the share price on the exercise date** – this is the best estimate possible

The total **difference** between the exercise price and assumed future share price (**intrinsic value**) is then **spread** over time to match with the accounting expense recognised under IFRS 2 – an amount **up to the value of the accounting expense** is recognised as a deferred tax asset (SFP) and deferred tax credit (P&L) as the entity benefits from future tax deductibility – any **excess** deferred tax benefit above the accounting expense is recognised directly in **equity**

See also our Deferred tax notes on **page 38**.

Possible methods to determine the fair value of an equity-settled share option

Black-Scholes model

Binomial model

Monty Carlo simulation

Share-based payment schemes with a choice of settlement (equity-settled or cash-settled)

Counterparty has the choice over how the scheme is settled

Apply **split accounting** – the entity has issued an instrument with a **debt** component insofar as the recipient may demand **cash** and an **equity** component so far as the recipient may demand settlement in **equity** instruments

First measure the **fair value** of the **debt** component – the **equity** component will then be a **residual** or **balancing** amount.

Example

A scheme allows the counterparty to choose between 10,000 shares (shares option) or cash to the value of 9,000 shares (cash option) on the grant date. The market price of the entity's shares on the grant date is £20 and the fair value of a share option on the grant date is £19.

In this case, the fair value of the cash route is 9,000 x £20 market price or £180,000 whilst the fair value of the share route is 10,000 x £19 or £190,000.

Therefore the fair value of the debt element is £180,000 (cash route) and the balancing fair value of the equity component under split accounting is £10,000 (£190,000 - £180,000).

Share-based payment – equity-settled

Finally, treat the **debt** element like a **cash-settled scheme** with the usual **spreading** approach and **taking into account** changes in fair value each year – treat the **equity** element like an **equity-settled scheme** with the **usual spreading approach** and **not taking into account** changes in fair value each year

Entity has the choice over how the scheme is settled

Treat as a **cash-settled** scheme to the extent it has a **present obligation** to deliver **cash** e.g. the entity is **prohibited** from issuing **shares** or has a **stated policy** or **past practice** of issuing **cash** rather than **shares**

If **no present obligation** to deliver **cash** exists, the entity should treat the transaction as a purely **equity-settled** transaction – if this equity treatment is applied but **cash is actually paid on settlement**, the cash should be treated as a **repurchase** of the **equity instrument** by a **deduction against equity**

Share-based payment – payment for goods and services

Suggested mark allocation in an FR question (CR Q2): 3 marks

Note – this scenario relates to a situation where a **supplier** is paid in the form of the entity's own shares rather than with cash or via a payable – it does not relate to a scenario involving an **employee's share options**

Treatment

State that the transaction is within the scope of IFRS 2

State that it is an "equity settled" transaction because the entity has received goods in exchange for an issue of shares

This type of transaction should be measured at the **fair value of the goods and services received** and **not** at the value of the **shares** themselves

> Therefore look out for an examiner trick – **the fair value of the entity's shares does not matter** – it is the **fair value of the goods and services** which is used

The journal entries should be

Dr Expenses (e.g. consultancy costs, purchases)

Cr Equity

There should not be recognition of any payable here – the credit entry should be to Equity as the entity will not be paying cash but rather shares or **equity**

Increase share capital by the nominal value of shares and place any excess into Share premium

Example – the entity obtains services with a fair value of 70,000 in exchange for shares with a nominal value of 20,000 and a fair value of 100,000

Debit	Expenses	70,000
Credit	Share capital	20,000
Credit	Share premium (balance)	50,000

The fair value of the shares is ignored – the fair value of the goods or services is what is considered

Example

A consultant provide services with a FV of 50,000 but is paid in the form of the entity shares which are worth 75,000 – use the figure of 50,000 to recognise this transaction

Tip – again, use the **FV** of the **goods and services** – ignore the FV of the **shares** offered in return

Share-based payment – Share Appreciation Rights

Suggested mark allocation in an FR question (CR Q2): 3 marks

This kind of instrument is deemed to be cash-settled as there is no issue of shares (therefore not equity-settled)

The treatment is similar to a cash-settled scheme i.e. **do** consider **updates in FV** at each year end

Non-market conditions

These conditions should be taken into account

Continued employment through to the vesting date will almost certainly be a condition of the scheme and is a non-market-based condition which must be considered

Treatment

Liability created in the SFP and an **expense** is recognised in the P&L

FV is re-measured each reporting date, taking into account the number of employees who are expected to qualify

Share-based payment – share options – summary of treatment

Suggested mark allocation in an FR question (CR Q2): 6 marks

See also **page 179** for cash-settled schemes and **page 180** for equity-settled schemes.

Treatment

Identify **whether cash-settled** or **equity-settled** and briefly **explain** the **reasons** for your choice of classification

Cash-settled

Remember to state why you are treating the scheme as cash-settled

Recognise an expense over the period that the related services are provided – for example, straight line over 3 years if the employee is required to work for 3 years before settlement of the incentive

The expense is based on the FV of the options – for a cash-settled scheme (and not for an equity-settled scheme) you should take into account changes in the FV of the options each year

> To find this year's charge, use the latest available FV but then look back to see what was already charged – do not go back and change any prior figures but **deduct amounts already recognised** as an expense or liability in prior years when calculating this year's charge

Remember to use a spreading fraction such as 1/3 in year 1 of a 3 year scheme, 2/3 in year 2 of a 3 year scheme, and so on – but then also allow for the amounts recognised in the prior year

Debit employment expenses and Credit a liability account (probably non-current but check) with the expense for the year

> Again, with a **cash-settled** scheme you use the **latest available FV** to find the cumulative expense and cumulative credit to liabilities but to find this year's debits and credits you need to deduct off any amounts already recognised in prior years

(This final stage is not necessary with an equity-settled scheme because the FV never changes once the scheme starts so you can just use the same amounts every year.)

Equity-settled

Remember to state why you are treating the scheme as equity-settled

Record an annual expense in profit or loss, spread over the vesting period with a corresponding annual increase in equity – IFRS 2 does not state where in equity the Credit arises: many companies add it to retained earnings

Measure each option at the FV at the grant date

Remove the year end estimate of total leavers over the whole vesting period from the calculation of the expense – we are only interested in allowing for the staff who are estimated to be in place at the time that the share options can be exercised

Share-based payment – share options – summary of treatment

Market-based vesting criteria (based on changes in the share price) should not be considered each year as the estimates of FV will already have taken these movements into account in the valuation model – therefore it does not matter whether the target is or is not met at the year end

Non-market-based vesting criteria (such as a profit target or margin target) should be considered at each year end to determine if vesting is probable – use the existing information as the best estimate of the likely scenario at the vesting date

Example first year calculation – remember to replace the figures with your information!

500 employees x 60% expected to remain x 100 options per employee x £3 FV x 1/5 vested

You do not need to write the words "employees", "expected to remain", "options per employee", "FV" or "vested" when writing the calculation into your answer – we have only included these for tutorial purposes

If you are looking at the second or later year, you would use a fraction such as 2/5, 3/5 and so on at the end of the calculation – compare this with all previous amounts already expensed in previous years to determine the net expense and incremental updating net credit to equity for the year you are looking at

See also   Share-based payment – cash-settled   p179

Share-based payment – equity-settled   p180

Social and environmental reporting

Companies Act 2006 requires **quoted** companies to include information on **environmental**, **employment** and **social** issues as part of the business review contained in the Directors' Report

From 1 October 2013, **quoted** companies must also report on **greenhouse gas emissions** in their Directors' Report

Unquoted companies are **encouraged** to provide this information **voluntarily** as **best practice**

Auditor considerations

It is possible that the audit firm has not been involved in assurance regarding social and environmental report before

The firm should ensure that it has **relevant expertise and resources** to complete the assignment

An **engagement letter** should be used to **clarify responsibilities** as these are **not defined by law**

It is **permissible** to provide **other services** (such as assurance over social and environmental reporting) under **ethical guidance for** auditors but the firm should consider the **level of the fee** to be received and ensure that the firm is **not economically dependent** on the client

The **social and environmental report** is expected to be included in the **same document** that contains the **audited financial statements**

If any of the **proposed assertions** are found to be **inconsistent** with the audited financial statements and management **refuses** to resolve the issue we would need to consider what impact this would have on the **auditor's report** and **whether** we should **continue the audit engagement**

Staff bonuses

Suggested mark allocation in an FR question (CR Q2): 2 marks

Constructive obligations

Past practice or an **announcement** will create a **constructive obligation** – this is treated as a **provision** as it is an **obligation** relating to a **past event**

Calculate the provision based on the number of employees expected to claim the bonus, using the scheme criteria e.g. 50 employees x 5% bonus rate x salaries

Dr Staff expenses (P&L)

Cr Provisions (SFP)

Employer's **National Insurance** at 13.8% would also be due on a bonus – remember that as the bonus (plus employer's National Insurance) would be tax deductible a tax saving would also be possible (e.g. actual cost would be **1 - tax rate** times the pre-tax cost) – CR is **not** a **tax exam** so mention these 2 points very **briefly**

The bonus should only be recognised when there is a **constructive** or **legal** obligation to make payment

This could relate to **conditions** in a related **contract** or could be based on **past practice**

Remember to look out for **time apportionment**

Treasury shares

Suggested mark allocation in an FR question (CR Q2): 2 marks

Tip – this question is not worth many marks so must be done **quickly** but at the same time it is **quite easy to score all the marks available** as the answer never varies from our points noted below

Points to mention

Equity instruments reacquired are known as Treasury shares

These are deducted from equity and shown as a separate (negative) reserve

Original share capital and share premium amounts remain unchanged

No gain or loss should be recognised on the issue, sale, purchase or cancellation of Treasury shares

Notes

Notes

Notes

Notes

Notes

Notes

Feedback

We hope that you found this book useful – we can only improve our learning materials and tuition services with your feedback so please feel free to get in touch at **getqualified@acasimplified.com**.

www.acasimplified.com

Printed in Great
Britain
by Amazon